MY LAI 4

MY LAI 4

a report
on the massacre and
its aftermath

Seymour M. Hersh

Random House New York

In memory of

ROBERT M. OCKENE

Contents

Preface

*T*HIS book is based primarily on interviews with
the men of Charlie Company who participated in
the attack on My Lai 4 on March 16, 1968. These
interviews inevitably produced a maze of conflicting stories: many of the men were unable to agree
on details, especially when asked to discuss an event
that took place nearly two years earlier and one in
which they may have committed premeditated murder.

I tried to balance that disadvantage three ways.

First, I interviewed as many members of the
company as possible to find those facts and incidents that were generally agreed upon. More than
fifty interviews were conducted with ex-GIs between
November, 1969, and February, 1970, involving
more than 50,000 miles of air travel. (A fact-finding
trip to Vietnam also was planned, but I canceled it
after the Army announced on December 7, 1969,
that it had impounded all of the pertinent field records of Charlie Company and that none would be
made available to journalists.) Many Charlie Company members were personally interviewed two or

more times, and most were contacted again by telephone to clarify conflicting points. Every witness and the date and place of the interview are cited in the "Notes" at the close of the book.

Second, I was provided access to a limited number of transcripts of interrogations by key witnesses that were conducted by the Criminal Investigating Division (C.I.D.) and the office of Inspector General, the two Army agencies which did the bulk of the investigation into My Lai 4.

Third, simply trying to ensure that my interviews were accurately reported was not enough, and I decided to censor some statements either because they were obviously contradictory or could not be verified by other witnesses. Where there was a conflict on significant points, that conflict is described as fully as possible.

Some GIs who were interviewed did not want their names used. Their wishes were respected, although I felt free to use some of their information when it was not about the events of that day. There are no anonymous quotations on any important details of the My Lai 4 operation itself. Some government officials, who agreed to discuss aspects relating to the subsequent investigation and prosecution of the case against Charlie Company, are not cited for obvious reasons.

The author gratefully acknowledges Ronald L. Ridenhour's permission to reproduce portions of the letter that initiated the investigation of My Lai 4. The public information officers at the Pentagon answered all queries with promptness and integrity. At Random House, Robert D. Loomis, my editor, and Bertha Krantz constantly provided the right advice at the right time.

Finally, I'd like to thank David Obst of Dispatch News Service in Washington for his help in getting the story of My Lai 4 to the public.

Seymour M. Hersh

Washington, D.C.
February 25, 1970

MY LAI 4

1

"You Wouldn't Believe It"

*I*T must have been a beautiful area, Quang Ngai Province, before the war. Situated on the northeast coast of South Vietnam, its green rice paddies and fertile farmlands stretch in a plain from the rolling foothills of the Ammanese Mountains east to the smooth white sand beaches of the South China Sea.

But the mountains—at some points less than ten miles inland—also provided a perfect haven for revolutionaries. The people of Quang Ngai have a history of rebellion dating back to the sixteenth century; and it was there that Vietminh troops led revolts against the French in the 1930s and after World War II; it was there that the Viet Cong fought the Saigon government in the 1950s and 1960s.

When Vietnam was partitioned in 1954, after the defeat of the French, Saigon officials estimated that 90,000 southerners went north to join the Hanoi regime. More than 90 percent of them came from Quang Ngai and a neighboring province. By the

mid-1960s Quang Ngai's population was estimated at 640,-
000; it was South Vietnam's third largest province. It was
also considered the toughest Viet Cong stronghold in the
country.

Attempts to separate the Viet Cong from the people had
begun in earnest early in 1962, when the Saigon government launched its Strategic Hamlet Program, later known
as "pacification" or "rural construction." Whole families
were uprooted and moved into fortified hamlets; if they
refused to go, units of the South Vietnamese army burned
their homes and fields. The program was a failure; it em-
bittered the peasants and did little to drive the Viet Cong
out of the area. Those civilians living inside fortified hamlets were still in contact with the National Liberation Front,
the political arm of the Viet Cong, and the gates and walls
of strategic hamlets were often scribbled over with Viet
Cong slogans of defiance.

Quang Ngai, not unnaturally, became the target for the
first major American combat operation of the Vietnam war.
The mission, conducted by the U. S. marines in 1965, was
called "Operation Starlight" and more than 700 Viet Cong
were reported killed. General William C. Westmoreland,
commander of the U. S. forces in Vietnam, later boasted
that the marines "could meet and beat any force they might
encounter."

The marines were given the job of freeing Quang Ngai
and its people from Communist control. In order to effect
this, a new concept of pacification was devised. As explained by a senior officer in early 1966: "We've been told
by our superiors that in many areas there isn't any chance
of pacifying the people, so instead we've got to sanitize our
region—kill the Viet Cong and move the civilians out. We
are not going to be able to make the people loyal to our
side. So we are going to sterilize the area until we can win

it back." American military men began quoting Mao Tse-tung to the effect that in guerrilla warfare the guerrillas are the fish and the people are the water. The officers talked of catching the fish by removing the water.

By this time much of Quang Ngai—as well as many other provinces—had been declared a "free-fire zone," in which all civilians were automatically suspected of being Viet Cong or Viet Cong sympathizers. The U. S. forces did not need to get approval from Saigon or local officials before staging bombing missions and artillery attacks. Tens of thousands of tons of bombs, rockets, napalm and cannon fire were poured into the free-fire zones periodically during 1965, '66 and '67. Frequently a pilot who would find himself left with some bombs or other ordnance after completing a routine mission would simply drop them on any likely-looking target. Artillery units devised a fire concept known as "harassment and interdiction," in which rounds of artillery were fired at irregular intervals at no targets in particular.

Yet the Viet Cong continued their hold on Quang Ngai.

In the spring of 1967 a new task force was assembled under command of the marines and ordered anew to sanitize the Communists in the area. Known as Task Force Oregon, it included two infantry brigades, one airborne unit and a brigade of Korean marines. In four months of military operations, Task Force Oregon claimed a kill of 3,300 Viet Cong, and said it had captured 800 weapons and arrested 5,000 suspects in the area. By then, as a side effect of the two years of U. S. operations in Quang Ngai, at least 138,000 civilians had been made homeless and brought into refugee camps, and about 70 percent of the dwellings in the province had been destroyed by bombs, shells or fire. Some infantry platoons formed a "Zippo squad"—named after the cigarette lighter—to handle the burning of homes during sweeps over hamlets. By the fall of 1967 the only government hospital in the province was treating more than 700 patients a month in its 400-bed facility. Hundreds of patients were overcrowding wards and corridors; hundreds more could not get in.

In September combat operations in Quang Ngai were handed over to a newly formed unit known as the Americal Division, which was composed of three brigades—the 196th, which had served as part of Task Force Oregon, and two new fighting units, the 11th Brigade from Schofield Barracks, Hawaii, and the 198th Brigade from Fort Hood, Texas. Many of the senior officers of the new division came from Fort Hood expressly to serve in the new headquarters, under the command of Major General Samuel W. Koster. A West Pointer, Koster had the rare opportunity to put together his own command staff, and selected a number of his classmates and friends to serve with him.

There were many rag-tag aspects to the new division. It was not an elite fighting force, and thus did not warrant having the helicopters and armored equipment of an airborne division or cavalry brigade. There was serious squabbling and competition among the three brigades that made up the division; many men chose to wear the patch of their brigade and not the new division patch. Competition was especially high in 1967–68 among the units over the number of enemy killed, or body count. For many brigade and battalion officers of the new division, Vietnam was a chance to put in some combat duty, earn battle ribbons, then come home with the combat experience they thought was vital to future promotion. At the time the desire to see combat was so high among the field grade officers—majors and above—that command experience was limited to six months.

The majority of troops in the front-line combat units were draftees. They knew little about Vietnam and usually cared less. And although ranking officers would deny it in public, they themselves had little use for the average combat GI. One former Americal Division colonel, talking about the GIs in one of the division's task forces, said, "When you talk to a bunch of task-force nothings—you're talking about a bunch of guys who don't know anything. They're dumb dogfaces." Another Vietnam officer added, "We are at war with the ten-year-old children. It may not be humanitarian, but that's what it's like."

In 1968 the Army's effort to educate GIs on the rights of prisoners consisted of two hours of instruction a year. Those GIs who were assigned to South Vietnam got several more lectures on the subject upon arrival, plus a wallet-sized card entitled "The Enemy in Your Hands," which told soldiers: "Always treat your prisoners humanely."

The average GI's ignorance of Vietnamese customs was appalling, but even more appalling was the fact that the Army's efforts to give the men some kind of understanding of what they would be faced with were minimal. The Vietnam-bound soldiers were given—at the most—only one or two lectures on the country and its people while in training.

Miss Claire Culhane, a Canadian who served as a volunteer in a tuberculosis hospital in Quang Ngai City in 1967–68, described how GIs assigned to pacification projects would often complain that the Vietnamese didn't care about their own children. They would say that the mothers tried to leave them behind when they were being evacuated. "Saw it with my own eyes," one GI said. "A woman hopped up on the chopper after setting her baby down on the ground. When I picked it up and handed it to her, she shouted and pointed to the ground and wouldn't accept the baby from me." The GI didn't know that a peasant woman in Quang Ngai believes it is unlucky to carry a baby across a threshold, and so she always sets the baby down, steps across, and then reaches back and picks it up—in a single swift movement. Another GI claimed that "you can't help these dinks. They like to live like pigs in hovels, and even when you build them new houses, they won't live in them." What *he* didn't know, however, was that according to the custom in that area, married women had to live in houses with full, double-sloped roofs. The new GI-built units had attached, single-slope corrugated tin-roofed huts. Since most of the peasant women were married, they refused to move into them.

Even worse than the misunderstandings were the deliberate cruelties and implicit assumptions of superiority on the part of the Americans. The pacification policy called for the free provision of medical care and medicines to the civilian population. But in practice, visits by medical teams to any hamlet were generally infrequent, and only a two-day supply of medicine would be given each patient in fear that the excess would fall into Viet Cong hands. Vietnamese were provided with new names when they entered a U. S. military hospital so the staff would have less trouble identifying them. Thus a civilian who had lost an eye was called, for example, "Bubbles," "Ohio," or "Cyclops." All U. S. hospitals had to keep 35 percent of their beds empty in case of an emergency involving American casualties; this rule was adhered to even in areas where the local civilian populace was in desperate need of medical help. Few Americans paid any attention to the names of hamlets and villages —many of them centuries old—and devised their own titles, which often found their way onto official military maps.

Young GIs soon learned that there were Army names for Vietnamese too: gook, dink and slope. One battalion commander in Vietnam named his helicopter the "Gookmobile" and listed his kills on the fuselage with a neatly painted row of conical hats. A general called his helicopter the "Slope-toter."

Many officers stalked Vietnamese in the free-fire zones from the air, shooting at anyone who moved below. One brigade commander ran a contest, and celebrated his unit's 10,000th enemy kill by giving the GI who shot him a week's pass to stay in the colonel's luxurious—by Vietnam standards—personal quarters. Many battalions staged contests among their rifle companies for the highest score in enemy kills, with the winning unit getting additional time for passes. Not every officer liked what he was doing. "I am sickened by the numbers of people we have killed and kept killing all year," one troop commander, after completing a tour of Vietnam in 1968, told a reporter. "This is not my concept of a soldier's career, just killing, killing, killing." But he did it nonetheless.

Among the highly touted colonels in Vietnam in 1967–68 was George S. Patton III, son of the famous World War II leader, who was commander of the 11th Armored Cavalry Regiment just south of Quang Ngai. His unit had the motto: "Find the bastards and pile on." He would exhort his men before combat by telling them, "I do like to see the arms and legs fly." He once told his staff, "The present ratio of 90 percent killing to 10 percent pacification is just about right." Patton celebrated Christmas in 1968 by sending cards reading: "From Colonel and Mrs. George S. Patton III—Peace on Earth." Attached to the cards were color photographs of dismembered Viet Cong soldiers stacked in a neat pile.

A military physician who served with Patton said, "In my experience, Patton was neither the best nor the worst of the military there. He is simply the product of the misbegotten and misguided idea that a single-minded dedication to destruction is to be highly rewarded." The doctor recalled that during his days with Patton's unit, two Vietnamese women on bicycles were run down and killed by a U. S. helicopter. The Army later exonerated the pilot. When Patton left Vietnam, he threw a farewell party at which he frolicked with a peace medallion around his neck while carrying the polished skull of a Viet Cong with a bullet hole above the left eye. When a congressman later read an account of that party and of some of Patton's statements in *The New York Times Magazine,* he privately wrote the Pentagon to complain. He received a reply twenty days later from a major general, airily brushing aside the congressman's concern and giving a candid view of the leeway provided combat officers in Vietnam:

> Colonel Patton was commanding a unit in combat. In carrying out his mission he properly had the safety and well-being of his men in mind. This concern is dramatized by consideration of the fact that his regiment averaged eight to ten average enemy contacts each week, inflicting heavy casualties on the enemy at a very low cost to his own men. In discussions with the members of his regiment he emphasized that combat was a kill-or-be-killed environment and used the phrase that he liked to see arms and legs fly to point this up.

> At a party given in his honor on the occasion of his departure from Vietnam, he was presented with a peace medallion. This medallion is the unofficial insignia of the platoon of the 11th Armored Cavalry Regiment that had the best combat record of any unit in the regiment. He was also presented with an old skull that obviously had been retrieved from the jungle.

In September, 1969, Colonel Patton's promotion to brigadier general of the U. S. Army was approved by the U. S. Senate. He was one of the youngest officers to achieve that high rank. Another fast-rising young officer was also up for promotion in 1969. Colonel Robert M. Montague served as a deputy for pacification to the military command in Saigon, and had volunteered to stay many years beyond his normal tour of duty. He was considered by the civilian pacification experts to be a source of continuity and strength among the military in South Vietnam. "He was a politically perceptive guy," one pacification worker said, "but he was controversial. He kept on telling the Army that it wasn't accomplishing its objective with its tactics." Montague also was what was known in the Army as a "5 percenter," an officer who did well at West Point and climbed in rank far ahead of his classmates. He was passed over for elevation to general in 1969.

To the inexperienced GIs and their inexperienced officers, life seemed cheap in Quang Ngai. "If you can shoot artillery and bombs in there every night," one Americal Division soldier said, "how can the people in there be worth so much?" A favorite joke heard repeatedly among the marines in Quang Ngai went something like this: The loyal Vietnamese should all be taken and put out to sea in a raft. Everybody left in the country should then be killed, and the nation paved over with concrete, like a parking lot. Then the raft should be sunk.

Some of the contempt was inevitable, a by-product of trying to conduct military operations in an area controlled by the Viet Cong by night, and no one by day. As many as one third of the Americal Division's casualties in some periods resulted from enemy mines and booby traps. The Viet Cong were always hard to find for the troops of the Americal Division, but the people were not. Bombs and artillery were now being called in to destroy villages in retaliation for sniper fire—or reports of sniper fire. The Vietnamese reciprocated the contempt. One British photographer traveled with units of the Americal in late 1967, and wrote: "In other parts of the country, children would quite often grin at you and beg gum. Not in Quang Ngai. They wouldn't look you in the eyes. They would hiss the Americans, and it upset the young conscripts, who'd been told to expect a great welcome from the people they were defending."

The infantry's basic tactic by then was a refined search-and-destroy method known informally as the scorched-earth policy. The technique was best described in a letter sent home by a GI to his family and later published in his local newspaper:

Dear Mom and Dad:

Today we went on a mission and I am not very proud of myself, my friends or my country. We burned every hut in sight!

It was a small rural network of villages and the people were incredibly poor. My unit burned and plundered their meager possessions. Let me try to explain the situation to you.

The huts here are thatched palm leaves. Each one has a dried mud bunker inside. These bunkers are to protect the families. Kind of like air raid shelters.

My unit commanders, however, chose to think that these bunkers are offensive. So every hut we find that has a bunker, we are ordered to burn to the ground.

When the ten helicopters landed this morning, in the midst of these huts, and six men jumped out of each "chopper," we were firing the moment we hit the ground. We fired into all the huts we could. Then we got "on line" and swept the area.

It is then that we burn these huts and take all men old enough to carry a weapon and the choppers come and get them. . . . Everyone is crying, begging and praying that we don't separate them and take their husbands and fathers, sons and grandfathers. The women wail and moan.

Then they watch in terror as we burn their homes, personal possessions and food. Yes, we burn all rice and shoot all livestock.

Some of the guys are so careless! Today a buddy of mine called *"La Dai"* (Come here) into a hut and an old man came out of the bomb shelter. My buddy told the old man to get away from the hut, and since we have to move quickly on a sweep, just threw a hand grenade into the shelter.

As he pulled the pin the old man got excited and started jabbering and running toward my buddy and the hut. A GI, not understanding, stopped the old man with a football tackle just as my buddy threw the grenade. . . . After he threw it, and was running for cover, we all heard a *baby* crying from inside the shelter.

There was nothing we could do. . . .

After the explosion we found the mother, two children (ages about six and twelve, boy and girl) and an almost newborn baby. That is what the old man was trying to tell us!

Such victims were often included in the day's statistics as enemy kills. The GIs in Quang Ngai had a joke for that practice, too: "Anything that's dead and isn't white is a VC."

What, perhaps, would happen inadvertently in the beginning became routine. Terry Reid of Fond Du Lac, Wisconsin, spent much of 1968 serving with the 11th Brigade of the American Division near Chu Lai, the division headquarters a few miles north of Quang Ngai City. The indiscriminate slaughter of Vietnamese women and children was commonplace in his unit. "Our company was credited with hundreds of kills," Reid said. "In the first fire fight our company encountered, my platoon alone accounted for forty kills. Yet no one in my platoon saw a [Viet Cong] body. But I witnessed many civilians being shot down like clay pigeons."

On one assault, Reid said, some GIs were killed in a mine

accident and his unit retaliated by killing sixty civilians—
women, children and old men: "After all this was done,
word came up from the captain at the rear that no women
were to be shot. If they don't clarify this—'No women are
to be shot'—it is free game." He explained that all young
Vietnamese "are supposed to be in the army. If you see
one and he is not . . . he is free game to be shot." One
day, he added, "we saw a young man in a rice paddy with
a water buffalo. Since he did not belong there, one of our
men shot him. We found no gun near him, but he wasn't
supposed to be there.

"After you kill your first innocent civilian, you tell yourself you are doing the right thing. Everyone else is doing it,
so you do it, too. You know you are doing it and can't turn
back." Reid remembered one GI who refused to carry out
an order, believing he would be imprisoned and sent out
of the unit. He was court-martialed, busted a few grades in
rank and sent back to rejoin his old platoon.

"To me," the ex-GI said, "the war was being ambushed
every three to five days, being left with scores of wounded
GIs, and then coming right back at the enemy by going
into an innocent village, destroying and killing people."

Reid spoke out in November, 1969, only after he had
read accounts of how another element of his brigade—the
11th—had perpetrated the wholesale slaughter of the village
of My Lai 4 northeast of Quang Ngai City. Before seeing
the news stories, Reid said, he had tried to put it all out
of his mind.

Most GIs simply weren't talking about such things earlier.

When *The New Yorker* magazine correspondent Jonathan
Schell was touring Quang Ngai Province in the late summer
of 1967—as he wrote later—a GI who was driving him
around in a jeep suddenly turned and said, "You wouldn't
believe the things that go on in this war."

"What things?" Schell asked.

"You wouldn't believe it."

"What kind of things, then?"

"You wouldn't believe it, so I'm not going to tell you," the GI said, shaking his head no. "No one's ever going to find out about some things, and after this war is over, and we've all gone home, no one is ever going to know."

2

Charlie Company

CHARLIE Company, 1st Battalion, 20th Infantry, came to Vietnam in December, 1967. Its men, like GIs in all combat units, considered themselves to be part of the best and toughest outfit in the newly formed 11th Brigade, which since December, 1966, had been readying itself for Vietnam at the Schofield Barracks, Hawaii. When the orders came to move out, Charlie Company was named to lead the advance party.

Captain Ernest L. Medina, the thirty-three-year-old former enlisted man who was the company's commanding officer, was proud of his men: "We became the best company in the battalion. We took every award—athletics, the company-of-the-month trophy." Medina's hustle had earned him the nickname "Mad Dog," a term that many of his company used when complaining about the captain's love of marching and field duty. Originally the nickname was meant as a compliment; Medina's men were wiping out a mock Communist aggressor unit during exercises in Hawaii when one officer broke in on the radio to proclaim, as he thought a Viet Cong might, "Hey, Mad Dog Medina." After that Medina would walk into the officers' club and people would say, "Hey, Mad Dog, how are you?" Medina took it as a joke.

The captain was enthusiastic about killing Viet Cong, even in mock battles. He was anxious to go to Vietnam to help win a war he believed in. But there was a personal reason, too—his career. A Mexican-American, he was born into poverty at Springer, New Mexico, in 1936. His mother died when he was an infant and he was raised in a hard-working ranching and farming community in Montrose, Colorado, on the western slope of the Colorado Mountains. When he was sixteen he lied about his age to enlist in the National Guard, and then the Army; from the very first he wanted to make the military a career. In 1964, after eight years in the infantry, he became an officer, graduating with honors from the Officers' Candidate School at Fort Benning, Georgia, and stayed on for two years to serve as an instructor. He wrote a school paper on "Meteorological Effects on the 4.2-in. Mortar Shell." In 1966 he was promoted to captain and made a company commander. By all accounts he was an excellent officer. Lieutenant Colonel Edward C. Beers, who served above Medina as commanding officer of the 1st Battalion in Hawaii and in Vietnam, personally considered him the most outstanding officer in his command: "He is a good Army man."

Medina's promotion to captain had been quick and easy, but rising to major would be more difficult because, as he said, he "didn't have enough education." Vietnam offered him his best chance, and he wanted to make the most of it.

He was off to a good start. Putting together a first-rate fighting unit was no easy feat in 1966. As always, the men assigned to infantry units were those who upon entering service performed poorly on the various Army qualification and aptitude examinations. GIs scoring average and above were usually assigned to a support or training unit, becoming, for example, clerk-typists or computer technicians. In Vietnam, there were as many as eight support troops for each combat soldier in the field.

Most of the men in Charlie Company had volunteered for the draft; only a few had gone to college for even one year. Nearly half were black, with a few Mexican-Americans. Most were eighteen to twenty-two years old. The favorite reading matter of Charlie Company, like that of other line infantry units in Vietnam, was comic books. Thirteen of the 130 men had not done well enough in the Army's basic intelligence tests to qualify for service, but had been accepted under a new program, Project 100,000, endorsed by Secretary of Defense Robert S. McNamara, which provided remedial education for those who would otherwise not be eligible for the Army. But as it worked out, none of the Project 100,000 men in Charlie Company had been exposed to any further education before getting shipped to Vietnam.

There was a decided advantage for Medina in not having a group of college graduates under his command: Charlie Company was a "grunt" unit; its men were the foot soldiers, the "GI Joes," who understood they were to take orders, not question them. In Hawaii, Medina had been fair but tough, handing out disciplinary penalties when needed but sticking up for his men on many occasions. Charlie Company respected and admired its captain. "He did everything for his men," Henry Pedrick, Jr., of Alameda, California, said. "When we had chow in the field, the enlisted men ate before the officers . . . all the time. His men always came first." Michael Bernhardt of Franklin Square, New

York, was impressed by Medina's "tremendous grip on his men. He was so hard-core." According to William Wyatt of Oklahoma City, Medina could outwalk anybody in the company: "He was hard. That's the way you got to do it."

Nobody in the unit, however, admired Medina as much as William L. Calley, Jr., then a twenty-four-year-old second lieutenant from Miami who was serving as a platoon leader. Medina was swarthy and powerfully built, and he commanded respect; Calley was boyish-looking, five-foot, three-inches tall, and unsure of himself. No sergeant would dare cross Medina in public; but Calley's chief noncommissioned officer, Sergeant Isaiah Cowen, a thirteen-year veteran from Columbia, South Carolina, was always arguing with Calley in front of the men.

Despite these differences, Calley and Medina had this in common: they both wanted to make the military a career. Calley had flunked out of Palm Beach Junior College in 1963 after earning four F's. By his own admission, he came from an emotionally cold family, one that had never been close. His high school friends had called him "Rusty," a nickname that stayed with him. There was nothing relaxed about him; he began smoking three to four packages of cigarettes a day and by the age of nineteen he was treated for a stomach ulcer. After leaving college, Calley worked as a bellhop and then briefly as a restaurant dishwasher before becoming a switchman for the then strike-bound East Coast Railway. He made the local newspapers in 1964 when police in Fort Lauderdale, Florida, arrested him for allowing a forty-seven-car freight train to block traffic for nearly thirty minutes during rush hour at several downtown intersections. He was cleared after a hearing.

Facing a bleak future, Calley saved some money, bought a car, and in 1965 left Florida, heading west. His friends didn't hear from him again for nearly three years; some

thought he was dead. He wandered around for a year—
one of his jobs then was taking photographs for an insurance
adjustment agency—before enlisting in the Army in July,
1966, while in Albuquerque, New Mexico. He quickly found
roots as an enlisted man, and was pleased when the Army,
despite his poor academic record, decided he would make a
good officer. He graduated from the Officers' Candidate
School at Fort Benning without even learning how to read
a map properly.

If there is any consensus among former members of
Calley's platoon in Vietnam, it is amazement that the Army
considered Calley officer material. Allen Boyce of Bradley
Beach, New Jersey, an eighteen-year-old rifleman at the
time of the massacre, said that "everybody used to joke
about Calley. He was one of those guys they just take off
the street." Rennard Doines of Fort Worth, Texas, thought
that Calley constantly tried to impress Medina: "He was
always trying to be the big man; always would be the one
to beat them [Vietnamese] up. He didn't know what was
going on half the time." Charles W. Hall of Columbus,
Ohio, was one of Calley's machine gunners: "Calley also
reminded me of a kid, a kid trying to play war." Hall added
that Calley, apparently trying to impress his men, once told
them that he had worked as a private detective in Miami—
perhaps thinking of his work for an insurance adjuster. "We
all called him 'Surfside 5½,' " a reference to a once-popular
television private-eye series known as *Surfside 6*.

Many men in the company recalled that Medina would
sometimes refer to Calley as "Sweetheart"; some thought
it was a mocking reference, others described it as just a
nickname. Gary Garfolo of Stockton, California, felt that
Medina "didn't show any respect for Calley; it was kind of
hard for anybody else to show respect." Roy L. Wood of
Richmond, Virginia, a rifleman in Calley's platoon, believed

that "Medina didn't like Calley. Calley was always doing things wrong . . . never right. I wondered sometimes how he got through OCS; he couldn't read no darn map and a compass would confuse his ass." Robert E. Maples of Freehold, New Jersey, said that Calley was always trying to "do things that would make him out to be a hero. That's what he tried to do—be a good boy in front of the captain. I just couldn't make it out . . . why he always had to try to make something out of himself he wasn't. He was always trying to be the first one."

Daniel E. Zeigler of Santa Barbara, California, served with Calley's platoon until he, Zeigler, was seriously injured in a mine accident in mid-February. He said that the men in his platoon mocked the young officer but followed his orders. A favorite Calley expression was "I'm the boss." Sergeant Cowen, a Negro who argued bitterly about tactics with Calley throughout their stay in Vietnam, commented that Calley "was my superior officer and I had to follow him whether I wanted to or not. Personal opinions don't enter into it: you can't have any ifs, ands, or buts about it, you have to go with your officers." The other key sergeant in the first platoon,* David Mitchell, of St. Francisville, Louisiana, was also a Negro.

In Charlie Company, the whites and blacks usually kept to themselves, as happened in most units in Vietnam. To Roy Wood, a black Southerner, "it seemed like some of those whites didn't want to be bothered too much with us." Other Negroes noted that Medina surrounded himself with whites in his headquarters group, the GIs who manned the

---

* Infantry companies theoretically are composed of three rifle platoons and a weapons platoon, each with forty men. The platoons, led by lieutenants, have four ten-man squads, each led by sergeants. Each squad is composed of two small-weapons fire teams. By the time Charlie Company went into My Lai 4, its ranks were depleted and most of the platoons were operating with two or three squads.

radios and helped run the company. Harry Stanley, born in Gulfport, Mississippi, a quick-witted Negro, had learned Vietnamese on his own while in Vietnam; in fact, he was convinced that he could speak Vietnamese more fluently than white members of the company who had studied it in Army language school. Yet it was not until Medina left the company in July, 1968, that Stanley got a chance to demonstrate this ability. On the whole, however, Charlie Company saved its antagonism for the Vietnamese. "There wasn't any prejudice in that whole company," said Herbert Carter of Houston, Texas, a Negro. "The government ought to take some pictures of us and say, 'Hey, these guys got along good—at least they killed together.' "

If there was any reason for what began to happen to Charlie Company, it was not too much combat—but too little. The company had conducted some search-and-destroy missions around 11th Brigade headquarters at Duc Pho shortly after arriving in Vietnam, with no real enemy contact. Its expectations rose when the brigade, with more units arriving every day from Hawaii, took over responsibility from the South Korean marines for monitoring an area forty miles to the north. The 150-square-mile area included parts of the embattled Quang Ngai Province east of Highway One to the South China Sea coast. To continue search-and-destroy operations in the zone, the brigade set up Task Force Barker, a tiny ad hoc unit composed of one company from each of the three battalions in the brigade. The parent unit of this force, headed by and named after Lieutenant Colonel Frank A. Barker, Jr., was the Americal Division operating out of Chu Lai to the south. Medina's company was assigned to the Task Force, and relocated on January 26, 1968, at Landing Zone Dotti, one of the three artillery bases from which the three companies worked and bivouaced in the area. One of the Task Force's main objectives would be keeping pressure on an area a few miles northeast of Quang Ngai known as "Pinkville," the name deriving from the fact that its higher population density caused it to appear in red on Army maps. The operation was given the code name "Muscatine."

"We were informed that the Viet Cong had been in the area for twenty to twenty-five years," Medina said. "The inhabitants in the outlying villages had all been moved at one time or another. The area was a permanent free-fire zone." The captain maintained that he routinely explained to his troops that if they received fire from a hamlet, they could return it, taking care not to fire at unarmed citizens who posed no seeming threat. At least one soldier recalled other advice. Gary Garfolo said that "Medina used to always tell us about the grenade bit. If you shoot a gook and check him out and find he's got an ID [identification card indicating he is not a Viet Cong]—plant a grenade on him."

But still nothing happened. Ronald Grzesik of Holyoke, Massachusetts, thought they "seemed to be blessed. I could walk along a street and not draw a shot—and other companies would come along the same street and get into a good fire fight. Other guys would be getting like, you know, hero treatment."

Occasionally the company, still new to Vietnam, was stunned by the evidence of the almost barbarous attitude veterans displayed toward the Vietnamese. Gregory Olsen, of Portland, Oregon, remembered that soon after they were in Vietnam they saw an American troop carrier drive by with "about twenty human ears tied to the antenna. It was kind of hard to believe. They actually had ears on the antenna."

Impatient for action, Charlie Company began to make a little of its own. Daniel Zeigler said that at first there was very little manhandling of civilian suspects: "It started off easy, then it got rough." Both Medina and Calley began trying to convince the company that most of the suspects in the area were Viet Cong. "Once Grzesik gave a prisoner something to eat, and they got mad." Zeigler never understood why Medina or Calley would beat a prisoner to try to get information in a language they couldn't understand anyway. "Whenever we got to a village, there were usually no males of military age around. So if they found one, they would just assume he was a VC. That is, if he wasn't an old man or a little teeny kid."

After many weeks of no combat, the company began to systematically beat its prisoners, and it began to be less discriminating about who was—or was not—a VC. Michael Bernhardt thought that as far as Medina was concerned, "Everything that walked and didn't wear any uniform was a VC. . . . He was as much of a nut as anybody else. He was pissed off at the people and had no respect for them." The lack of respect was apparently infectious. "On the lower level," Charles Hall said, "squad leaders and platoon leaders didn't enforce the rules—like for beating people. This happened every day; every day there was disregard for the people. There were a few people who made a habit of this."

Charlie Company got its first ear early in January near Duc Pho. While on patrol, a GI had seen four Viet Cong in a valley below. Medina called in artillery, and sent a squad in after the bombardment to search for the dead. Harry Stanley saw them come back "with an ear. Medina was happy; it was his first kill." Some members of the company, finding ears of Viet Cong hard to come by, began marking their estimated kills with notches on their rifles.

Charlie Company had an isolated life, staying either in the field or at one of the artillery fire bases. Unless there was an operation in a village, the men saw only whores, beggars and thieves. "They were all after my money, I'll tell you that," said James R. Bergthold of Niagara Falls, New York. He quickly learned to direct his anger at all Vietnamese: "Why shouldn't I? They were the enemy."

Eusebio B. Santellana of San Antonio, Texas, had served with Charlie Company since December, 1967; he watched as his buddies got shredded by mines. (Later he lost a leg in Vietnam, but Santellana was not at My Lai 4: he had been called home in early March, 1968, on an emergency leave.) He remembered the company's feelings then about the Vietnamese, and his own: "I hope they kill everybody over there, because they won't tell you where the VC is. They should kill every goddamn thing over there—VC, animals . . . You can slap them around but they won't tell you— and then the VC snipe at you. Villagers won't tell you nothing. How come they won't tell you? They ought to know. How come they don't like GIs?"

He said the trouble in Vietnam was that "the people aren't straight like we are. We ask them something and they don't know. After we leave, the VC hit us. They all look alike."

Danny Zeigler recalled, with a touch of shame, one operation in early February in which the first platoon grabbed and beat up four old men they knew were not Viet Cong: "I looked at it then and I looked at myself. Most of the guys realized what was happening. It wasn't so much that we were against the people as it was . . . just a ridiculous thing, all of it, everything.

About a week after the company arrived at LZ Dotti, Lieutenant Calley ordered Michael Bernhardt to shoot at a running woman. He half-heartedly ran after her, yelling, "*Dong lai*"—the Vietnamese expression for "Stop"—but she got away. Calley berated him for not firing. Bernhardt later contemplated asking other officers in the unit about the propriety of such an order, but decided not to; he was sure Calley would deny everything, and Bernhardt would just end up with a reputation as a troublemaker. "I would just fire and miss on purpose after that."

During these weeks, Medina said, the company was learning that "this was a dangerous area"—mines and booby traps, often placed by women and children, were everywhere. This was a prevalent belief among GIs in Vietnam, including Charlie Company, yet not one member of Charlie Company who was asked could cite a specific act of terror by either a woman or a child. Such incidents most certainly did occur throughout Vietnam, and still do, but they weren't happening to Charlie Company. When one of its men got hurt, there was usually one reason: carelessness.

One of the first casualties at LZ Dotti was Zeigler: "We were coming back from a night ambush, and I stepped off the trail and got wounded." The date was February 14, 1968. Zeigler decided that what happened to him "could be considered dumb in a way. We were using a well-worn trail and that would be dumb." Something else dumb happened that day: there was no medic around. Calley, who was leading the operation, had forgotten to take one along. "It was our first night patrol, and we asked him for one. I guess he just didn't think it was necessary." Zeigler suffered twenty-one punctures in his body from mine fragments, including a collapsed lung. Luckily, the incident took place a few hundred yards from Dotti, and medical help came before he could bleed to death.

A few days later Medina led his men into the Song My area northeast of Quang Ngai City, establishing a blocking position while other Task Force Barker units sought the Viet Cong's crack 48th Battalion, then operating nearby. By this time the three rifle platoons of Charlie Company were rotating patrols. The second platoon was in the field cautiously making its way toward the river when it contacted the enemy. It was a tough fight, Medina told someone later, with intense small-arms and rocket fire. Michael Bernhardt's squad was a few hundred meters behind the others: "Somebody yelled 'incoming'— it was in front of us. I sat down on a dyke, lit a cigarette and watched the battle going on. I saw these guys shooting; I couldn't figure it out; it was really confusing. Nobody knew what was going on." But Bernhardt watched as one nearby GI fired his M16 rifle at a group of Vietnamese civilians crouching in a rice paddy fifteen feet in front of the men. "The moment the rounds were incoming, this guy let the people have it . . . They fell down right fast." The GI approached them. "They were holding their ID cards over their heads. Then he said 'Okay' and the people walked away." It had been a family of four, Bernhardt realized—a mother, father, child and infant. The infant was left behind in the field; it had been struck by one of the GI's bullets.

A few soldiers in the squad near the river were hit by rifle fire from the well-entrenched Viet Cong on the other side. The second platoon was further shaken when mortar shells, flinging showers of shrapnel, injured a few more men. Gunships were called in. "They held them under fire and we took off," Bernhardt recalled, "running back for a mile or so. Then we kind of pulled ourselves together and walked the rest of the way." Gary Crossley of San Marcos, Texas, another member of the second platoon, confirmed that his unit had been overwhelmed. "We had to take off running," he said. "We didn't have a chance." Bernhardt blamed the company officers for the debacle. "It was always ridiculous. They'd sit down and try to figure out what to do next, and it would be over before they figured it out."

On the next day Lieutenant Calley led his first platoon

back into the area and again there was enemy fire. Calley was visibly upset when interviewed about the event: "It was a good all-day battle. We received quite a bit of fire. We got hit quite badly. I had my radio operator shot up under me. It was our first time in there and we just literally got the shit shot out of us. So we pulled back, digged up replacements. That was my first good taste of it."

None of Calley's fellow platoon members saw the battle as anywhere near that awesome. Most considered what happened—the death of William Weber, a radioman—simply another result of the lieutenant's stupidity.

Ron Grzesik, Weber's best friend and bunkmate, remembered the incident clearly: "Up until this time, we really never ran into the enemy too much. As far as contact, nothing special, nothing resembling a battle or even a hard fight." He said that the platoon was moving along the river toward a small hamlet when the snipers opened up. "We got pinned down but we made it into the village. Calley called in a lot of artillery." (Others said that Medina had suggested that Calley remain in the village or carefully withdraw in order to avoid exposing his men to fire.) The platoon pulled out, "moving straight back away from the river, using the river as cover." The snipers opened up again, but the men, crawling shoulder-deep through muck and mud, escaped injury. "We got four hundred or five hundred meters away from the river and the snipers weren't bothering us too much. Then we started moving back toward the river, walking toward a causeway. I thought Calley was lost again." To make it worse, instead of ordering the men to walk in a four-foot-deep dyke alongside the river, Calley permitted them—by this time the company was strung out in single file—to walk on top of it. "I laid this on stupidity," Grzesik said. "Our own stupidity and our being green. We hadn't been in Vietnam too long."

It was then that Weber got hit. Robert Maples overheard Calley and Cowen decide to put off telling the company that Weber had been killed. The platoon had been vigorously complaining about going back to the river; the news that a man had been killed because of it would perhaps cause panic. "You figured," Maples said, "like Weber got shot and you don't know if it was going to be you next. You can't have a platoon leader who's trying to make things look good. You can't put yourself out for people like that. He [Calley] was jeopardizing his people, their lives and whatnot, just for his reputation. The whole thing was stupid to me."

The platoon blamed the Viet Cong for Weber's death. Describing the incident twenty months later, Sergeant Cowen said that the platoon had been pinned down by fire from the Song My area across the river; he said that gunships were needed to get the platoon out safely. Weber was the unit's only reported casualty that day, yet Charles A. West, of Chicago, a member of the third platoon, told how his unit— rushing to the aid of Calley's platoon—went "two or three times . . . to the water's edge and harassed the village with gunfire. Each time we got wounded men."

The incident served to heighten the hostility of the company for the Vietnamese. By this time the men had been living in the field for nearly three weeks without relief; they were tired, confused, and morale was low. Olsen said that the company "always seemed to get the dirty job. Everybody thought that we were getting the short end of the stick." Some were beginning to wonder whether they were being volunteered for additional search-and-destroy duty by Captain Medina, who told the men that the Viet Cong were afraid of Charlie Company and knew what a good unit it was: that's why they had yet to come out and engage it in a fire fight. The men of Charlie Company were getting more violent, Olsen said, routinely kicking away the Viet-

namese children who would come begging for gum or
money when the unit went through villages and hamlets.
William Doherty of Reading, Massachusetts, talked about
the dirt and grime of living in the field: "We had to rip
our pants up to get a change of clothes." The company
routine in the field was fixed: the men would awake at
dawn, eat a cold C-ration breakfast, pack up, move, walk
until lunch, eat a cold C-ration lunch, walk again until
dinner. Sometimes they would have yet another C-ration
meal, but more often helicopters would fly in a hot meal to
the unit or take the men back into LZ Dotti for dinner.
"But after dinner," Doherty said, "they'd fly us out again to
set up camp for the night." Richard Pendleton of Richmond,
California, felt the company was "kept away from everything. People were made kind of backwards. We never got
to the beach places; our job was different. They just kind
of snuck us in the back way and put us in the field. They
tried to put it into our minds that this is our job—to do this.
After a while, people just kept to themselves."

Michael Terry, a Mormon from Orem, Utah, said that
the company simply treated the Vietnamese "like animals. A
lot of guys didn't feel that they were human beings." Charles
Sledge, of Batesville, Mississippi, knew why the Vietnamese
were beginning to show increasing hostility to the young
GIs: "We did it ourselves. We would go through a village,
tear up stuff, kicking it over, burning it down—I know.
I did it."

The company was taking its cue from Captain Medina,
who was quick to beat and terrorize suspected Viet Cong
soldiers or civilian sympathizers in his attempt to gain intelligence information. John T. Paul of Cherry Hills, New
Jersey, one of Medina's radiomen, described the captain's
interrogation technique. "He thought that if you could in-
still fear in a prisoner, you'd most likely get them to talk.

He wanted to put a point across right away on these people—'We're not fucking around with you.'" Sometimes
Medina's antics brought laughs. Paul recalled that Medina
once hid behind a large rock after hearing that one of the
platoons was bringing up an old man—a "papa-san"—for
questioning. "He told us to 'watch this' and then jumped out
with a roar and grabbed the guy in a bear hug from behind.
They started rolling on the ground. The old man was
screaming." He already had been gashed on the head with
the gunsight from a rifle. The old man, helpless with fear,
defecated, much to the merriment of the company. With another prisoner, Medina suddenly pulled out "his survival
knife and cut the guy a little behind the ear." The old man
wasn't a Viet Cong, so the company medic patched him up,
gave him a cigarette and sent him on his way. "A lot of this
was done in jest," Paul added. Herbert Carter got fed up
with the war and the people at this point. "I used to like kids
—but I can't stand them any more . . . kinks and slant-
eyed people. I didn't like them—and the CO didn't either."

The captain was even irritated by the incongruous appearance of young Vietnamese entrepreneurs during combat
assignments. "We'd be out on a mission," Gary Garfolo explained, "and all of a sudden a dozen kids would come
selling Cokes and sandwiches. I mean we were *out on a
mission*. Medina would come and chase them away, kick
them in the ass, throw them out of there."

The atrocities began with Carter. About mid-February
Charlie Company was assigned another patrol mission in
the Task Force area. As they filed through a hamlet, Carter
offered a "papa-san" a cigarette. As the man took it, Carter
suddenly began to club him with his rifle butt. He broke his
jaw and ribs. Most of the company watched. Some "were
mad as hell," Olsen said, but no one said anything. Nor was

Carter reprimanded. Later that day the first platoon separated to reconnoiter on its own. By this time, Harry Stanley recalled, the platoon had the idea that "if they wanted to do something wrong, it was always all right with Calley. He didn't try to stop them." A few hours later two men in the platoon suddenly began firing at a figure walking across a field. They said he was carrying something. It took twelve shots with an M16 rifle before he fell. They ran forward and shot again. The victim turned out to be a woman farmer who was carrying the deed to her land in a tube. Stanley was asked to translate the writing for Lieutenant Calley, and then listened as the lieutenant radioed Captain Medina and told him his men had killed a Viet Cong.

A few minutes later two men, possibly Viet Cong guerrillas, were brought in to Calley. This time he turned to Grzesik—who had had 350 hours of Vietnamese language instruction while the company was in Hawaii—to interpret. But he was interrupted, Grzesik said, when "somebody brought in an old man. He was a farmer; there was no doubt in my mind." Grzesik questioned the man, quickly found that he had an identification card. "I told Calley I didn't think he was a VC." But it didn't matter; the first platoon hadn't had any contact with the enemy in weeks. Calley motioned Grzesik away with his M16. "Why are you going to kill him?" Grzesik asked. Calley told him to "get moving." But before Calley could fire, Herbert Carter moved forward.

Harry Stanley was ten feet away. During an interrogation in October, 1969, he told the Army's main police unit, the Criminal Investigation Division (C.I.D.), what happened next: "Carter hit the old man into a well, but the old man spread his legs and arms and held on and didn't fall . . . Then Carter hit the old man in his stomach with his rifle stock. The old man's feet fell into the well, but he continued to hold on with his hands. Carter hit the man's fingers, trying to make him fall . . . and Calley shot the man with his M16."

Carter talked easily about the incident in an interview. "Bergthold captured the old man," he said. "I was the one that threw him into the well. We tried to make him talk and he wouldn't. After we tried, I picked him up and threw him in the well—then Lieutenant Calley blew his brains out. I started to shoot him myself," he added. "I just said, 'The hell with this tramp'—you know what I mean. He was a VC."

According to Grzesik, Calley then radioed Captain Medina and told him that "an old man jumped in a well and we got him." Calley told his commanding officer the man was a Viet Cong guerrilla. Medina promptly asked Calley to have the well carefully searched to make sure it wasn't part of an enemy tunnel system. No one in the company would crawl into the—by now—bloody well. Calley reported it was not part of a tunnel complex.

Bergthold was asked what made him bring in the old man for questioning. "I found him working in a rice paddy," he said. Did he think he could be a Viet Cong? "I don't know . . . you never know."

On February 25 Charlie Company suffered its worst day. Six men were killed and twelve seriously wounded when it ran into a well-laid minefield north of Pinkville. Most of the casualties were in the first and third platoons. Medina earned the Silver Star, the Army's third highest medal for valor, for his role in rescuing the wounded. "I lost some of my best men that day," Medina said. The incident stunned the company. Carter recalled that "the guys were confused. They said, 'Okay, you guys [the Viet Cong] want to be tough. We can be rough right with them.' The VC were blowing us up with mines—sending little kids with grenades. It was getting ridiculous."

The shock of the incident was increased for a few by the nagging thought that perhaps it could have been avoided. Allen Boyce said that it happened when "we was in a hurry and had to move through the minefield." Sergeant Cowen was leading the platoon that day, and Boyce thought he could have taken his time and gone around the minefield, which was marked on the maps: "A whole lot of guys were mad about it, mad at Sergeant Cowen." Michael Bernhardt remembered something else: the Task Force was operating in an area that formerly was the responsibility of the South Korean marines. He was convinced the mine that ruptured the company had been emplaced by the Koreans. "We all knew it, you see"—meaning that the Koreans didn't always clear their minefields or report them, as regulations required. The incident happened, Bernhardt continued, "in a place where the Koreans had laid mines out in their perimeter. But the guys in the company didn't want to know the sad truth. They were all for the Army; all gung ho. Someone you can blame is the Viet Cong or the Vietnamese. Somebody you can't blame are the big men in the Army. They [the men in Charlie Company] didn't want to believe it . . . They knew it. We all talked about it. The truth is that the Koreans had set up a base camp and surrounded it with mines. And we walked into the area that they had set up."

About this time at least two members of Charlie Company had begun to assault and abuse Vietnamese women. Some of the younger members of the company were troubled by this, but no punishment was apparently meted out. On one occasion a few GIs accosted a woman working in a field in a friendly area. According to Michael Bernhardt, they took away her baby and then "they raped her and killed her . . . I guess they killed her baby, too." One of the group was busy taking photographs with an Instamatic camera during the incident.

Medina and his men continued their fruitless routine of search-and-destroy missions until the second week in March, when the company was assigned relatively easy guard duty near LZ Dotti. Olsen and Paul Meadlo of Terre Haute, Indiana, an easygoing farm boy, were guarding a bridge together near Pinkville. "We did nothing but laugh and run around," Olsen said. Meadlo was a particular company favorite. The GIs often teased him when they saw a water buffalo, yelling, "Hey, Paul, there's another cow."

On March 14, two days before the mission to My Lai 4, a small squad from the third platoon ran into a booby trap. Gary Garfolo watched Sergeant George Cox lead a patrol into a cluster of trees. Suddenly he heard Cox call over the radio that he'd found something. "Next thing—kaBOOM— big mushroom cloud, everybody hits the ground. We went over there—this big ruin of a place—and found everybody tore up." Richard Pendleton arrived seconds after the booby trap went off: "Somebody that was injured said Cox picked the bomb up before it went off. He was kind of curious about those things." Cox was killed and one GI lost his eyes, an arm and a leg. There were screams and calls for medics. Michael Terry was also on the patrol: "It was a kind of a gruesome thing. We were good and mad." Charles West recalled that "guys were going around kicking sandbags and saying, 'Those dirty dogs, those dirty bastards.' "

The wounded and dead were lifted away by helicopters, and the remaining men in the squad—about eight—began marching back to LZ Dotti. En route they stole a radio while walking through a small hamlet. "We stole it because we wanted it," Gary Garfolo explained. "They had it and we wanted it—we figured, 'What the hell, they're gooks, they

caused Cox's death.' " "Everybody was just taking things,"
said Richard Pendleton. "They knew that people here might
have something to do with it." The squad wanted more revenge. Moments after leaving the hamlet, a GI shouted,
"Something's moving in the bushes." Lieutenant Jeffrey La
Crosse of the third platoon ordered them to find out what
it was. Someone yelled, "He's got a weapon. He's got a
weapon," and the squad opened up with M16 rifle fire. The
suspect fell, and the squad came running after him. William
Doherty saw what happened next: "I ran there. I was the
first to get there. I kicked her, and then I saw she was a
woman, so I stopped. But some of the other guys kept on."
Michael Terry yelled in protest as he came up to the group.
The woman was still alive. Someone suggested calling in a
helicopter to evacuate her to a hospital. "She don't need no
medivac," one GI suddenly exclaimed, and shot her in the
chest. Someone else stole her ring.

The murder and the theft of the radio and ring angered
the residents of the hamlet, a secure area near LZ Dotti.
They called in the Vietnamese national police. The police
began asking around at the LZ; eventually they found their
way to Charlie Company and Medina. "Medina was really
hot," Garfolo remembered. "Not because we did it, but because it got to him—we got caught." Garfolo doesn't know
whether the ring or radio was returned. No charges were
filed.

Medina later had a much different version of what had
happened. He told a reporter that the booby trap was deto-
nated by remote control and that his company found a fif-
teen-year-old girl hidden nearby with her hand still on the
plunger. His men then killed her, Medina said. He did not
mention any theft charges. "Captain Medina just kind of
hushed that up," Michael Terry said of the shooting of the

woman, "but something like that's a war crime, just out and out a war crime."

By now many in the company had given in to an easy pattern of violence. Some were still struggling. Ronald Grzesik had developed a fondness for his Vietnamese instructors at the Army language school in Hawaii. He was particularly impressed by a lieutenant colonel and a pretty woman teacher. "You get to like them. I had a little more respect for the average Vietnamese." Yet his attitude changed day by day in the weeks before the My Lai 4 assault: "It just started building. I don't know why. Everybody reached the point where they were frustrated. We weren't getting any action, yet the only thing on our mind was survival. After Bill [William Weber] got killed, I began to stop caring. I remember writing a letter home saying that I once had sympathy for these people, but now I didn't care. I became passive; I wouldn't beat them up but I wouldn't try to stop it. Yet I told Calley at one point that I wouldn't question anybody unless he stopped beating them up. There'd be days when I'd just be sick of it."

Others told of their agony in letters home. Gregory Olsen came from devout Mormon stock in Oregon; he didn't drink or smoke. A few days after My Lai 4 he and Mike Terry, also a Mormon, got special permission to leave the company and attend a Mormon conference at Da Nang. On March 14, a Thursday, Olsen had written the following letter to his father, Samuel G. Olsen, scrawled in pencil on standard GI stationery:

Dear Dad:

How's everything with you?

I'm still on the bridge, we leave here Saturday [for the My Lai 4 mission].

One of our platoons went out on a routine patrol today

and came across a 155-mm artillery round that was booby trapped. It killed one man, blew the legs off two others, and injured two more.

And it all turned out a bad day made even worse. On their way back to "Dotti" they saw a woman working in the fields. They shot and wounded her. Then they kicked her to death and emptied their magazines in her head. They slugged every little kid they came across.

Why in God's name does this have to happen? These are all seemingly normal guys; some were friends of mine. For a while they were like wild animals.

It was murder, and I'm ashamed of myself for not trying to do anything about it.

This isn't the first time, Dad. I've seen it many times before. I don't know why I'm telling you all this; I guess I just want to get it off my chest.

My faith in my fellow men is shot all to hell. I just want the time to pass and I just want to come home.

I really believe as you do, Dad, there is a cause behind all this, and if it is God's will for me to go, I would rather do it here than home on the Freeway.

Saturday we're going to be dropped in by air in an N.V.A. stronghold [My Lai]. I'm still hoping I'll be able to get out of here for a few days to go to a conference.

Don't expect any letters for a while but please keep writing them.

I love and miss you and Mom so much—

Your son,
Greg

On the day after the mine incident Charlie Company held a brief funeral service for Sergeant George Cox. By all accounts, it was a moving occasion. "The men were hurt real bad, real bad," Henry Pedrick said. "The company was very upset. The company was also very angry. It had revenge on its mind." Like other members of the company, Pedrick came close to tears as he talked about it.

After the chaplain's service Medina got up to speak. The men were quiet. Charles West was moved by what the captain told them: "He knew it was hard on them, but it was just as hard on him. Maybe he didn't show it because he was held responsible for being a leader, but that was no reason for the guys to hold back. He said to let it out, let it go." At this point, West said, many of the men of Charlie Company cried.

Medina then began to tell his men about the next day's mission. As Medina described it later, he and Colonel Barker had begun planning the mission early in the day. At one point they flew from LZ Dotti in a helicopter for a peek at My Lai 4, eleven kilometers to the south, being careful not to get too close and alert the enemy. Barker told Medina that elements of the 48th Viet Cong Battalion, one of the enemy's best units, with a strength of 250 to 280 men, was in My Lai 4. The colonel said intelligence reports predicted that the hamlet's women and children would be gone by 7 A.M., en route to the weekly markets in Quang Ngai City or Son Tinh District.* Charlie Company's mission was to destroy the 48th Battalion as well as My Lai 4.

Medina was ordered to burn houses and blow up bunkers and tunnels, along with killing the livestock. Normally, killing animals was not done, Medina said, but he didn't think it was unusual: "The idea was to destroy the village so the

---

* The basic administrative units in South Vietnam are, in order of size and importance, provinces, villages and hamlets. The Quang Ngai area is unique in that it also has sub-hamlets that are under the jurisdiction of nearby hamlets. According to the Pentagon, My Lai 4 was one of six numbered sub-hamlets of Tu Chung hamlet in the village of Song My. The hamlet's titles were confused even further by a U. S. Army map project that Americanized many of the original names. Some Vietnamese reportedly refer to My Lai 4 as Xom Lang.

48th VC would be forced to move. It looked like a tough
fight." The captain claimed that his men would be outnumbered at least two-to-one by the Viet Cong during the assault, but added that he did not expect heavy casualties. "I
have a lot of faith in the fire power that the American infantryman has. The helicopter pilots and the gunship pilots
do a tremendous job in supporting the infantryman on the
ground." *

Medina's objective in the pep talk after the funeral that
night, he later explained, was to "fire them up to get them
ready to go in there. I did not give any instructions as to
what to do with women and children in the village."

There were sharply conflicting opinions among the company over what Medina did order. Many thought the captain had ordered them to kill every person in My Lai 4.
Others thought that he had given routine—if more emotional—orders for a search-and-destroy mission. A few felt
that Medina had been vague, as if to leave the interpretation
of his orders for the next day up to the feelings and conscience of the individual soldier.

Harry Stanley told the C.I.D. that Medina "ordered us to
'kill everything in the village.' The men in my squad talked
about this among ourselves that night," Stanley said, "because the order . . . was so unusual. We all agreed that

* Despite Medina's confidence in the ability of helicopter gunships, there
is a puzzling aspect to Charlie Company's mission as outlined by him.
Most military tacticians, especially those in Vietnam, agree that an
attacking force must have a manpower superiority of at least three-to-one
over a well-armed enemy force defending fortified positions. Only sev-
enty to seventy-five GIs from Charlie Company took part in the assault
against the expected 250 to 280 Viet Cong guerrillas. Charlie Company
thus would actually have been outnumbered four-to-one. Even more
puzzling, then, were Medina's eventual decisions to attack the hamlet
by initially sending in only two platoons, and to land the company less
than 200 yards from My Lai 4, well within range of enemy rifle fire. The
inevitable question left begging is: Did Medina really expect to find
Viet Cong troops in My Lai 4?

Medina meant for us to kill every man, woman and child in the village." Charles West remembered hearing the captain say that when Charlie Company left the area "nothing would be walking, growing, or crawling." He also recalled the captain's saying that the women and children would be out of the area. Herbert Carter told the C.I.D. he thought Medina had been explicit. "Well, boys," he said the captain told them, "this is your chance to get revenge on these people. When we go into My Lai, it's open season. When we leave, nothing will be living. Everything's going to go." Sergeant Cowen testified (during an Army hearing in December, 1969, on criminal charges against Sergeant Mitchell, stemming from Mitchell's role at My Lai 4) that Medina "told us to destroy everything with life." He was asked if he took that to mean he was supposed to kill civilians. "Yes, sir," Cowen said. Charles Hall remembered Medina's saying, "Don't take any prisoners." Robert Maples recalled that Medina "told us everything in the village was the enemy. The way I think he said it—and the way they took it—was that anything in the village was VC." According to Michael Bernhardt, Medina said, "They're all VCs, now go in and get them. We owe them something . . ." Then Bernhardt added, "He didn't have to specifically say women and kids." The company interpreter, Sergeant Nguyen Dinh Phu of the South Vietnamese army, was told that night by one of the black GIs that Charlie Company was going to destroy a village and its people the next day. The interpreter assumed it was the usual GI bragging.

But Gregory Olsen was sure Captain Medina did not order the killing of women and children: "He did say—he did make the statement—that we had a score to even up. He did tell us that we were to go there and destroy the food supply and hamlet. He said it was known that VC sympathizers were in My Lai 4 and that it was harboring VCs. He told us to shoot the enemy." At this point someone asked, "Who is the enemy?" Olsen said Medina then defined "the enemy as anybody that was running from us, hiding from us, or who appeared to us to be the enemy. If a man was running, shoot him; sometimes even if a woman with a rifle was running, shoot her. He never at any time said, 'Slaughter the people.' " Ron Grzesik agreed with Olsen. He heard Medina tell the men "to go in and destroy the village; to make it uninhabitable," but did not recall an order to destroy the inhabitants.

Perhaps the best answer to what was said or what was believed was supplied by Henry Pedrick: "The orders could be interpreted in different ways to different persons according to their emotional structure . . . One person just might interpret it to kill if he wanted to." The question about who was the enemy was asked by Michael Terry. He thought the captain was in an awkward position because of the charged atmosphere following the funeral service. "Guys were asking when they would have a chance to fight instead of marching around and getting blown up. Some of the guys were all shook up, and like a good captain he was trying to appease them." The net result, Terry said, was that Medina "gave the impression—he never specifically said it—that they could kill the people . . . that they could kill anybody they saw. I remember paying attention to how he was handling the situation. It seemed like there would be a whole lot of killing the next day."

Most significantly, Lieutenant William Calley thought so, too. "Every time we got hit [in the Pinkville area] it was from the rear," Calley said later. "So the third time in there the order came down to go in there and make sure no one was behind us. Just to clear the area. It was a typical combat assault tactic," the young officer explained. "We came in hot [firing], with a cover of artillery in front of us, came down the line, and destroyed the village."

Bernhardt recalled that by March 16, "we'd already gone through some villages and the company more or less roughed up the people. If anybody ever told them to go there and kill everybody, they'd do it. They were looking for an excuse, and they got it."

For Ron Grzesik, My Lai 4 was the end of a vicious circle that had begun months earlier. "It was like going from one step to another, worse one," he said. "First, you'd stop the people, question them, and let them go. Second, you'd stop the people, beat up an old man, and let them go. Third, you'd stop the people, beat up an old man, and then shoot him. Fourth, you go in and wipe out a village."

3

The Day – Part I

*N*OBODY saw it all. Some, like Roy Wood, didn't even know the extent of the massacre until the next day. Others, like Charles Sledge, who served that day as Calley's radioman, saw more than they want to remember.

But they all remember the fear that morning as they climbed onto helicopters at LZ Dotti for the assault on Pinkville. They all remember the sure knowledge that they would meet face-to-face for the first time with the enemy.

Calley and his platoon were the first to board the large black Army assault helicopters. They were heavily armed, each man carrying twice the normal load of rifle and machine-gun ammunition. Leading the way was Calley, who had slung an extra belt of M16 rifle bullets over his shoulder. There were nine helicopters in the first lift-off, enough for the first platoon—about twenty-five men—and Captain Medina and his small headquarters unit of

three radiomen, some liaison officers and a medic. It was
sunny and already hot when the first helicopter started its
noisy flight to My Lai 4. The time was 7:22 A.M.; it was
logged by a tape recorder at brigade headquarters. A brief
artillery barrage had already begun; the My Lai 4 area was
being "prepped" in anticipation of that day's search-and-destroy mission. A few heavily armed helicopters were firing
thousands of small-caliber bullets into the area by the time
Calley and his men landed in a soggy rice paddy 150
meters west of the hamlet. It was harvest season; the green
fields were thick with growth.

The first platoon's mission was to secure the landing
zone and make sure no enemy troops were left to fire at
the second wave of helicopters—by then already airborne
from LZ Dotti. As the flight of helicopters hovered over
the landing area, the door gunners began spraying protec-
tive fire to keep the enemy—if he were there—busy. One
of the helicopter's pilots had reported that the LZ was "hot,"
that is, Viet Cong were waiting below. The first platoon
came out firing. But after a moment some men noticed
that there was no return fire. "I didn't hear any bullets
going past me," recalled Charles Hall, a machine gunner
that day. "If you want to consider an area hot, you got to be
fired on."

The platoon quickly formed a perimeter and secured the
landing zone. Sergeant Cowen spotted an old man. Sledge
was a few yards to Cowen's right: "We came to a well and
there was a VC. We thought it was a VC. He was standing
and waving his arms. Cowen fell back and said, 'Shoot the
so-and-so.' I fired once, and then my [rifle] magazine fell
out." Paul Meadlo noted that "the gook was standing up
shaking and waving his arms and then he was shot." Allen
Boyce saw it a little differently: "Some guy was in a rice
field, doing something to a rice plant. He looked up and

he got it. That was the most confused operation I ever went on. Just everything was screwed up."

By this time those Viet Cong who were in the area had slipped away. Some local supporters of the guerrillas also left, but they did not go too far. They watched as Charlie Company went through My Lai 4.

After about twenty minutes the second flight of helicopters landed, and the fifty men of the second and third platoons jumped off. Gary Garfolo heard the helicopter blades make sharp crackling sounds as they changed pitch for the landing. "It was a 'pop, pop, pop' sound like a rifle. Lots of us never even heard a hot LZ before. We knew we were going into a hot place. This got their adrenalin going." The men were quickly assembled. Calley's first platoon and Lieutenant Stephen Brooks' second platoon would lead the sweep into the hamlet—Calley to the south, and Brooks to the north. The third platoon, headed by Lieutenant Jeffrey La Crosse, would be held in reserve and move in on the heels of the other men. Captain Medina and his headquarters unit would move with the third platoon and then set up a command post (CP) inside to monitor the operation and stay in touch with other units. Charlie Company was not alone in its assault; the other two companies of Task Force Barker set up blocking positions to the north and south. They were there to prevent the expected Viet Cong troops from fleeing.

The My Lai 4 assault was the biggest thing going in the Americal Division that day. To get enough airlift, Task Force Barker had to borrow helicopters from other units throughout the division. The air lanes above the action were carefully allotted to high-ranking officers for observation. Barker monitored the battle from the 1,000-foot level. Major General Samuel Koster, commanding general of the division, was allotted the air space at 2,000 feet. His helicopter was permanently stationed outside his door at division headquarters twenty-one miles to the north, waiting to fly him to the scene of any action within minutes. Oran K. Henderson, commander of the 11th Brigade, was given the top spot—at 2,500 feet. All of the helicopters were to circle counterclockwise over the battle area. Flying low, beneath the 1,000-foot level, would be the gunships, heavily armed helicopters whose mission was to shoot down any Viet Cong soldiers attempting to escape.

Brigade headquarters, sure that there would be a major battle, sent along two men from the Army's 31st Public Information Detachment to record the event for history. Jay Roberts of Arlington, Virginia, a reporter, and photographer Ronald L. Haeberle of Cleveland, Ohio, arrived with the second wave of helicopters and immediately attached themselves to the third platoon, which was bringing up the rear.

The hamlet itself had a population of about 700 people, living either in flimsy thatch-covered huts—"hootches," as the GIs called them—or in solidly made red-brick homes, many with small porches in front. There was an east-west footpath just south of the main cluster of homes; a few yards further south was a loose surface road that marked a hamlet boundary. A deep drainage ditch and then a rice paddy marked the eastern boundary. To the south of My Lai 4 was a large center, or plaza area—clearly the main spot for mass meetings. The foliage was dense: there were high bamboo trees, hedges and plant life everywhere. Medina couldn't see thirty feet into the hamlet from the landing zone.

The first and second platoons lined up carefully to begin the hundred-meter advance into My Lai 4. Walking in line is an important military concept; if one group of men gets

too far in front, it could be hit by bullets from behind—
those fired by colleagues. Yet even this went wrong. Ron
Grzesik was in charge of a small first-platoon fire team of
riflemen and a machine gunner; he took his job seriously.
His unit was supposed to be on the right flank, protecting
Calley and his men. But Grzesik's group ended up on Calley's left.

As Brooks' second platoon cautiously approached the
hamlet, a few Vietnamese began running across a field
several hundred meters on the left. They may have been
Viet Cong, or they may have been civilians fleeing the
artillery shelling or the bombardment from the helicopter
gunships. Vernado Simpson, Jr., of Jackson, Mississippi,
saw a man he identified as a Viet Cong soldier running with
what seemed to be a weapon. A woman and a small child
were running with him. Simpson fired . . . again and
again. He killed the woman and the baby. The man got
away. Reporter Roberts saw a squad of GIs jump off a
helicopter and begin firing at a group of people running
on a nearby road. One was a woman with her children.
Then he saw them "shoot two guys who popped up from
a rice field. They looked like military-age men . . . when
certain guys pop up from rice fields, you shoot them." This
was the young reporter's most dangerous assignment. He
had never been in combat before. "You're scared to death
out there. We just wanted to go home."

The first two platoons of Charlie Company, still unfired
upon, entered the hamlet. Behind them, still in the rice
paddy, were the third platoon and Captain Medina's command post. Calley and some of his men walked into the
plaza area in the southern part of the hamlet. None of the
people was running away; they knew that U. S. soldiers
would assume that anyone running was a Viet Cong and
would shoot to kill. There was no immediate sense of panic.

The time was about 8 A.M. Grzesik and his fire team were a few meters north of Calley; they couldn't see each other because of the dense vegetation. Grzesik and his men began their usual job of pulling people from their homes, interrogating them, and searching for Viet Cong. The villagers were gathered up, and Grzesik sent Meadlo, who was in his unit, to take them to Calley for further questioning. Grzesik didn't see Meadlo again for more than an hour.

Some of Calley's men thought it was breakfast time as they walked in; a few families were gathered in front of their homes cooking rice over a small fire. Without a direct order, the first platoon also began rounding up the villagers. There still was no sniper fire, no sign of a large enemy unit. Sledge remembered thinking that "if there were VC around, they had plenty of time to leave before we came in. We didn't tiptoe in there."

The killings began without warning. Harry Stanley told the C.I.D. that one young member of Calley's platoon took a civilian into custody and then "pushed the man up to where we were standing and then stabbed the man in the back with his bayonet . . . The man fell to the ground and was gasping for breath." The GI then "killed him with another bayonet thrust or by shooting him with a rifle . . . There was so many people killed that day it is hard for me to recall exactly how some of the people died." The youth next "turned to where some soldiers were holding another forty- or fifty-year-old man in custody." He "picked this man up and threw him down a well. Then [he] pulled the pin from a M26 grenade and threw it in after the man." Moments later Stanley saw "some old women and some little children—fifteen or twenty of them—in a group around a temple where some incense was burning. They were kneeling and crying and praying, and various soldiers . . . walked by and executed these women and children by shooting them in the head with their rifles. The soldiers killed all fifteen or twenty of them . . ."

There were few physical protests from the people; about eighty of them were taken quietly from their homes and herded together in the plaza area. A few hollered out, "No VC. No VC." But that was hardly unexpected. Calley left Meadlo, Boyce and a few others with the responsibility of guarding the group. "You know what I want you to do with them," he told Meadlo. Ten minutes later—about 8:15 A.M.—he returned and asked, "Haven't you got rid of them yet? I want them dead." Radioman Sledge, who was trailing Calley, heard the officer tell Meadlo to "waste them." Meadlo followed orders: "We stood about ten to fifteen feet away from them and then he [Calley] started shooting them. Then he told me to start shooting them. I started to shoot them. So we went ahead and killed them. I used more than a whole clip—used four or five clips." There are seventeen M16 bullets in each clip. Boyce slipped away, to the northern side of the hamlet, glad he hadn't been asked to shoot. Women were huddled against their children, vainly trying to save them. Some continued to chant, "No VC." Others simply said, "No. No. No."

Do Chuc is a gnarled forty-eight-year-old Vietnamese peasant whose two daughters and an aunt were killed by the GIs in My Lai 4 that day. He and his family were eating breakfast when the GIs entered the hamlet and ordered them out of their homes. Together with other villagers, they were marched a few hundred meters into the plaza, where they were told to squat. "Still we had no reason to be afraid," Chuc recalled. "Everyone was calm." He watched as the GIs set up a machine gun. The calm ended. The people began crying and begging. One monk showed his identification papers to a soldier, but the American simply said, "Sorry." Then the shooting started. Chuc was wounded in the leg, but he was covered by dead bodies and thus spared. After waiting an hour, he fled the hamlet.

Nguyen Bat, a Viet Cong hamlet chief who later defected, said that many of the villagers who were eating breakfast outdoors when the GIs marched in greeted them without fear. They were gathered together and shot. Other villagers who were breakfasting indoors were killed inside their homes.

The few Viet Cong who had stayed near the hamlet were safely hidden. Nguyen Ngo, a former deputy commander of a Viet Cong guerrilla platoon operating in the My Lai area, ran to his hiding place 300 meters away when the GIs came in shooting, but he could see that "they shot everything in sight." His mother and sister hid in ditches and survived because bodies fell on top of them. Pham Lai, a former hamlet security guard, climbed into a bunker with a bamboo top and heard but did not see the shootings. His wife, hidden under a body, survived the massacre.

By this time, there was shooting everywhere. Dennis I. Conti, a GI from Providence, Rhode Island, later explained to C.I.D. investigators what he thought had happened: "We were all psyched up, and as a result, when we got there the shooting started, almost as a chain reaction. The majority of us had expected to meet VC combat troops, but this did not turn out to be so. First we saw a few men running . . . and the next thing I knew we were shooting at everything. Everybody was just firing. After they got in the village, I guess you could say that the men were out of control."

Brooks and his men in the second platoon to the north had begun to systematically ransack the hamlet and slaughter the people, kill the livestock and destroy the crops. Men poured rifle and machine-gun fire into huts without knowing —or seemingly caring—who was inside.

Roy Wood, one of Calley's men who was working next to Brooks' platoon, stormed into a hut, saw an elderly man hiding inside along with his wife and two young daughters: "I hit him with my rifle and pushed him out." A GI from Brooks' platoon, standing by with an M79 grenade launched, asked to borrow his gun. Wood refused, and the soldier asked another platoon mate. He got the weapon, said, "Don't let none of them live," and shot the Vietnamese in the head. "These mothers are crazy," Wood remembered thinking. "Stand right in front of us and blow a man's brains out." Later he vomited when he saw more of the dead residents of My Lai 4.

The second platoon went into My Lai 4 with guns blazing. Gary Crossley said that some GIs, after seeing nothing but women and children in the hamlet, hesitated: "We phoned Medina and told him what the circumstances were, and he said just keep going. It wasn't anything we wanted to do. You can only kill so many women and children. The fact was that you can't go through and wipe out all of South Vietnam."

Once the first two platoons had disappeared into the hamlet, Medina ordered the third platoon to start moving. He and his men followed. Gary Garfolo was caught up in the confusion: "I could hear heavy shooting all the time. Medina was running back and forth everywhere. This wasn't no organized deal." So Garfolo did what most GIs did when they could get away with it. "I took off on my own." He ran south; others joined him. Terrified villagers, many carrying personal belongings in wicker baskets, were running everywhere to avoid the carnage. In most cases it didn't help. The helicopter gunships circling above cut them down, or else an unfortunate group ran into the third platoon. Charles West sighted and shot six Vietnamese, some with baskets, on the edge of My Lai 4: "These people were running into us, away from us, running every which way. It's hard to distinguish a mama-san from a papa-san when everybody has on black pajamas."

West and his men may have thought that these Vietnamese were Viet Cong. Later they knew better. West's first impression upon reaching My Lai 4: "There were no people in the first part . . . I seen bodies everywhere. I knew that everyone was being killed." His group quickly joined in.

Medina—as any combat officer would do during his unit's first major engagement—decided to move his CP from the rice paddy. John Paul, one of Medina's radiomen, figured that the time was about 8:15 A.M. West remembered that "Medina was right behind us" as his platoon moved inside the hamlet. There are serious contradictions about what happened next. Medina later said that he did not enter the hamlet proper until well after 10 A.M. and did not see anyone kill a civilian. John Paul didn't think that Medina ever entered the hamlet. But Herbert Carter told the C.I.D. that Medina did some of the shooting of civilians as he moved into My Lai 4.

Carter testified that soon after the third platoon moved in, a woman was sighted. Somebody knocked her down, and then, Carter said, "Medina shot her with his M16 rifle. I was fifty or sixty feet away and saw this. There was no reason to shoot this girl." The men continued on, making sure no one was escaping. "We came to where the soldiers had collected fifteen or more Vietnamese men, women and children in a group. Medina said, 'Kill every one. Leave no one standing.'" A machine gunner began firing into the group. Moments later one of Medina's radio operators slowly "passed among them and finished them off." Medina did not personally shoot any of them, according to Carter, but moments later the captain "stopped a seventeen- or eighteen-year-old man with a water buffalo. Medina told the boy to make a run for it," Carter told the C.I.D. "He tried to get him to run but the boy wouldn't run, so Medina shot him with his M16 rifle and killed him . . . I was seventy-five or eighty meters away at the time and I saw it plainly." At this point in Carter's interrogation, the investigator warned him that he was making very serious charges against his commanding officer. "What I'm telling is the truth," Carter replied, "and I'll face Medina in court and swear to it."

If Carter was correct, Medina walked first into the north side of My Lai 4, then moved south with the CP to the hamlet plaza and arrived there at about the time Paul Meadlo and Lieutenant Calley were executing the first group of villagers. Meadlo still wonders why Medina didn't stop the shooting, "if it was wrong." Medina and Calley "passed each other quite a few times that morning, but didn't say anything. I don't know if the CO gave the order to kill or not, but he was right there when it happened . . . Medina just kept marching around."

Roberts and Haeberle also moved in just behind the third platoon. Haeberle watched a group of ten to fifteen GIs methodically pump bullets into a cow until it keeled over. A woman then poked her head out from behind some brush; she may have been hiding in a bunker. The GIs turned their fire from the cow to the woman. "They just kept shooting at her. You could see the bones flying in the air chip by chip." No one had attempted to question her; GIs inside the hamlet also were asking no questions. Before moving on, the photographer took a picture of the dead woman. Haeberle took many more pictures that day; he saw about thirty GIs kill at least a hundred Vietnamese civilians.

When the two correspondents entered My Lai 4, they saw dead animals, dead people, burning huts and houses. A few GIs were going through victims' clothing, looking for piasters. Another GI was chasing a duck with a knife; others stood around watching a GI slaughter a cow with a bayonet.

Haeberle noticed a man and two small children walking toward a group of GIs: "They just kept walking toward us . . . you could hear the little girl saying, 'No, no . . .' All of a sudden the GIs opened up and cut them down." Later he watched a machine gunner suddenly open fire on a group of civilians—women, children and babies—who had been collected in a big circle: "They were trying to run. I don't know how many got out." He saw a GI with an M16 rifle fire at two young boys walking along a road. The older of the two—about seven or eight years old—fell over the first to protect him. The GI kept on firing until both were dead.

As Haeberle and Roberts walked further into the hamlet, Medina came up to them. Eighty-five Viet Cong had been killed in action thus far, the captain told them, and twenty suspects had been captured. Roberts carefully jotted down the captain's statistics in his notepad.

The company's other Vietnamese interpreter, Sergeant Duong Minh, saw Medina for the first time about then. Minh had arrived on a later helicopter assault, along with Lieutenant Dennis H. Johnson, Charlie Company's intelligence officer. When he saw the bodies of civilians, he asked Medina what happened. Medina, obviously angry at Minh for asking the question, stalked away.

Now it was nearly nine o'clock and all of Charlie Company was in My Lai 4. Most families were being shot inside their homes, or just outside the doorways. Those who had

tried to flee were crammed by GIs into the many bunkers
built throughout the hamlet for protection—once the bunkers became filled, hand grenades were lobbed in. Everything
became a target. Gary Garfolo borrowed someone's M79
grenade launcher and fired it point-blank at a water buffalo:
"I hit that sucker right in the head; went down like a shot.
You don't get to shoot water buffalo with an M79 every
day." Others fired the weapon into the bunkers full of people.

Jay Roberts insisted that he saw Medina in My Lai 4
most of the morning: "He was directing the operations in
the village. He was in the village the whole time I was—
from nine o'clock to eleven o'clock."

Carter recalled that some GIs were shouting and yelling
during the massacre: "The boys enjoyed it. When someone
laughs and jokes about what they're doing, they have to be
enjoying it." A GI said, "Hey, I got me another one." Another said, "Chalk up one for me." Even Captain Medina
was having a good time, Carter thought: "You can tell when
someone enjoys their work." Few members of Charlie Company protested that day. For the most part, those who didn't
like what was going on kept their thoughts to themselves.

Herbert Carter also remembered seeing Medina inside
the hamlet well after the third platoon began its advance: "I
saw all those dead people laying there. Medina came right
behind me." At one point in the morning one of the members
of Medina's CP joined in the shooting. "A woman came out
of a hut with a baby in her arms and she was crying," Carter
told the C.I.D. "She was crying because her little boy had
been in front of their hut and . . . someone had killed the
child by shooting it." When the mother came into view, one
of Medina's men "shot her with an M16 and she fell. When
she fell, she dropped the baby." The GI next "opened up on
the baby with his M16." The infant was also killed. Carter

also saw an officer grab a woman by the hair and shoot her with a .45-caliber pistol: "He held her by the hair for a minute and then let go and she fell to the ground. Some enlisted man standing there said, 'Well, she'll be in the big rice paddy in the sky.' "

In the midst of the carnage, Michael Bernhardt got his first good look at My Lai 4. Bernhardt had been delayed when Medina asked him to check out a suspicious wood box at the landing zone. After discovering that it wasn't a booby trap, Bernhardt hurried to catch up with his mates in the third platoon. He went into the hamlet, where he saw Charlie Company "doing strange things. One: they were setting fire to the hootches and huts and waiting for people to come out and then shooting them. Two: they were going into the hootches and shooting them up. Three: they were gathering people in groups and shooting them. The whole thing was so deliberate. It was point-blank murder and I was standing there watching it. It's kind of made me wonder if I could trust people any more."

Grzesik and his men, meanwhile, had been slowly working their way through the hamlet. The young GI was having problems controlling his men; he was anxious to move on to the rice paddy in the east. About three quarters of the way through, he suddenly saw Meadlo again. The time was now after nine. Meadlo was crouched, head in his hands, sobbing like a bewildered child. "I sat down and asked him what happened." Grzesik felt responsible; after all, he was supposed to be a team leader. Meadlo told him Calley had made him shoot people. "I tried to calm him down," Grzesik said, but the fire-team leader couldn't stay long. His men still hadn't completed their sweep of My Lai 4.

Those Vietnamese who were not killed on the spot were being shepherded by the first platoon to a large drainage ditch at the eastern end of the hamlet. After Grzesik left,

Meadlo and a few others gathered seven or eight villagers in one hut and were preparing to toss in a hand grenade when an order came to take them to the ditch. There he found Calley, along with a dozen other first platoon members, and perhaps seventy-five Vietnamese, mostly women, old men and children.

Not far away, invisible in the brush and trees, the second and third platoons were continuing their search-and-destroy operations in the northern half of My Lai 4. Ron Grzesik and his fire team had completed a swing through the hamlet and were getting ready to turn around and walk back to see what was going on. And just south of the plaza, Michael Bernhardt had attached himself to Medina and his command post. Shots were still being fired, the helicopters were still whirring overhead, and the enemy was still nowhere in sight.

One of the helicopters was piloted by Chief Warrant Officer Hugh C. Thompson of Decatur, Georgia. For him, the mission had begun routinely enough. He and his two-man crew, in a small observation helicopter from the 123rd Aviation Battalion, had arrived at the area around 9 A.M. and immediately reported what appeared to be a Viet Cong soldier armed with a weapon and heading south. Although his mission was simply reconnaissance, Thompson directed his men to fire at and attempt to kill the Viet Cong as he wheeled the helicopter after him. They missed. Thompson flew back to My Lai 4, and it was then, as he told the Army Inspector General's office in June, 1969, that he began seeing wounded and dead Vietnamese civilians all over the hamlet, with no sign of an enemy force.

The pilot thought that the best thing he could do would be to mark the location of wounded civilians with smoke so that the GIs on the ground could move over and begin treating some of them. "The first one that I marked was a girl that was wounded," Thompson testified, "and they came over and walked up to her, put their weapon on automatic and let her have it." The man who did the shooting was a captain, Thompson said. Later he identified the officer as Ernest Medina.

Flying with Thompson that day was Lawrence M. Colburn, of Mount Vernon, Washington, who remembered that the girl was about twenty years old and was lying on the edge of a dyke outside the hamlet with part of her body in a rice paddy. "She had been wounded in the stomach, I think, or the chest," Colburn told the Inspector General (IG). "This captain was coming down the dyke and he had men behind him. They were sweeping through and we were hovering a matter of feet away from them. I could see this clearly, and he emptied a clip into her."

Medina and his men immediately began moving south toward the Viet Cong sighted by Thompson. En route they saw the young girl in the rice paddy who had been marked by the smoke. Bernhardt had a ground view of what happened next: "He [Medina] was just going alone . . . he shot the woman. She seemed to be busy picking rice, but rice was out of season. What she really was doing was trying to pretend that she was picking rice. She was a hundred meters away with a basket . . . if she had a hand grenade, she would have to have a better arm than me to get us . . . Medina lifted the rifle to his shoulder, looked down the barrel and pulled the trigger. I saw the woman drop. He just took a potshot . . . he wasn't a bad shot. Then he walked up. He got up real close, about three or six feet, and shot at her a couple times and finished her off. She was a real clean corpse . . . she wasn't all over the place, and I could see her clothing move when the bullets hit . . . I could see her twitch, but I couldn't see any holes . . . he didn't shoot her in the head." A second later, Bernhardt remembered, the captain "gave me a look, a dumb shit-eating grin."

By now it was past 9:30 A.M. and the men of Charlie Company had been at work for more than two hours. A few of them flung off their helmets, stripped off their heavy gear, flopped down and took a smoke break.

4

The Day – Part II

*H*UGH Thompson's nightmare had only begun with the shooting of the girl. He flew north back over the hamlet and saw a small boy bleeding along a trench. Again he marked the spot so that the GIs below could provide some medical aid. Instead, he saw a lieutenant casually walk up and empty a clip into the child. He saw yet another wounded youngster; again he marked it, and this time it was a sergeant who came up and fired his M16 at the child.

Larry Colburn, who was just eighteen years old at the time, noticed that "the infantrymen were killing everything in the village. The people didn't really know what was happening. Some of them began walking out of there and the GIs just started going up to them and shooting them all in the back of the head." He added, "We saw this one woman hiding there. She was alive and squatting; she looked up when we flew over. We dropped a smoke marker. When we came back she was in the same position

—only she was dead. The back of her head was blown off. It had to be point-blank."

Thompson was furious. He tried unsuccessfully to radio the troops on the ground to find out what was going on. He then reported the wild firings and unnecessary shootings to brigade headquarters. All the command helicopters flying overhead had multi-channel radios and could monitor most conversations. Lieutenant Colonel Barker apparently intercepted the message and called down to Medina at the CP just south of the plaza. John Kinch of the mortar platoon heard Medina answer that he "had a body count of 310." The captain added, "I don't know what they're doing. The first platoon's in the lead. I am trying to stop it." A moment later, Kinch said, Medina called Calley and ordered, "That's enough for today."

Harry Stanley was standing a few feet away from Calley near some huts at the drainage ditch when the call came from Medina. He had a different recollection: "Medina called Calley and said, 'What the fuck is going on?' Calley said he got some VC, or some people that needed to be checked out." At this point Medina cautioned Calley to tell his men to save their ammunition because the operation still had a few more days to run.

It is not clear how soon or to whom Medina's order was given, but Stanley told the C.I.D. what Calley did next: "There was an old lady in a bed and I believe there was a priest in white praying over her . . . Calley told me to ask about the VC and NVA and where the weapons were. The priest denied being a VC or NVA." Charles Sledge watched with horror as Calley pulled the old man outside: "He said a few more words to the monk. It looked like the monk was pleading for his life. Lieutenant Calley then took his rifle and pushed the monk into a rice paddy and shot him point-blank."

Calley then turned his attention back to the crowd of Vietnamese and issued an order: "Push all those people in the ditch." Three or four GIs complied. Calley struck a woman with a rifle as he pushed her down. Stanley remembered that some of the civilians "kept trying to get out. Some made it to the top . . ." Calley began the shooting and ordered Meadlo to join in. Meadlo told about it later: "So we pushed our seven to eight people in with the big bunch of them. And so I began shooting them all. So did Mitchell, Calley . . . I guess I shot maybe twenty-five or twenty people in the ditch . . . men, women and children. And babies." Some of the GIs switched from automatic fire to single-shot to conserve ammunition. Herbert Carter watched the mothers "grabbing their kids and the kids grabbing their mothers. I didn't know what to do."

Calley then turned again to Meadlo and said, "Meadlo, we've got another job to do." Meadlo didn't want any more jobs. He began to argue with Calley. Sledge watched Meadlo once more start to sob. Calley turned next to Robert Maples and said, "Maples, load your machine gun and shoot these people." Maples replied, as he told the C.I.D., "I'm not going to do that." He remembered that "the people firing into the ditch kept reloading magazines into their rifles and kept firing into the ditch and then killed or at least shot everyone in the ditch." William C. Lloyd of Tampa, Florida, told the C.I.D. that some grenades were also thrown into the ditch. Dennis Conti noticed that "a lot of women had thrown themselves on top of the children to protect them, and the children were alive at first. Then the children who were old enough to walk got up and Calley began to shoot the children."

One further incident stood out in many GIs' minds: seconds after the shooting stopped, a bloodied but unhurt two-year-old boy miraculously crawled out of the ditch, crying.

He began running toward the hamlet. Someone hollered, "There's a kid." There was a long pause. Then Calley ran back, grabbed the child, threw him back in the ditch and shot him.

Moments later Thompson, still in his helicopter, flew by. He told the IG what happened next: "I kept flying around and across a ditch . . . and it . . . had a bunch of bodies in it and I don't know how they got in the ditch. But I saw some of them were still alive." Captain Brian W. Livingston was piloting a large helicopter gunship a few hundred feet above. He had been monitoring Thompson's agonized complaints and went down to take a look for himself. He told a military hearing: "There were bodies lying in the trenches . . . I remember that we remarked at the time about the old Biblical story of Jesus turning water into wine. The trench had a grey color to it, with the red blood of the individuals lying in it."

By now Thompson was almost frantic. He landed his small helicopter near the ditch, and asked a soldier there if he could help the people out: "He said the only way he could help them was to help them out of their misery." Thompson took off again and noticed a group of mostly women and children huddled together in a bunker near the drainage ditch. He landed a second time. "I don't know," he explained, "maybe it was just my belief, but I hadn't been shot at the whole time I had been there and the gunships following hadn't . . ." He then saw Calley and the first platoon, the same group that had shot the wounded civilians he had earlier marked with smoke. "I asked him if he could get the women and kids out of there before they tore it [the bunker] up, and he said the only way he could get them out was to use hand grenades. 'You just hold your men right here,'" the angry Thompson told the equally angry Calley, " 'and I will get the women and kids out.' "

Before climbing out of his aircraft, Thompson ordered Colburn and his crew chief to stay alert. "He told us that if any of the Americans opened up on the Vietnamese, we should open up on the Americans," Colburn said. Thompson walked back to the ship and called in two helicopter gunships to rescue the civilians. While waiting for them to land, Colburn said, "he stood between our troops and the bunker. He was shielding the people with his body. He just wanted to get those people out of there." Colburn wasn't sure whether he would have followed orders if the GIs had opened fire at the bunker: "I wasn't pointing my guns right at them, but more or less toward the ground. But I was looking their way." He remembered that most of the soldiers were gathered alongside a nearby dyke "just watching. Some were lying down; some of them were sitting up, and some were standing." The helicopters landed, with Thompson still standing between the GIs and the Vietnamese, and quickly rescued nine persons—two old men, two women and five children. One of the children later died en route to the hospital. Calley did nothing to stop Thompson, but later stormed up to Sledge, his radioman, and complained that the pilot "doesn't like the way I'm running the show, but I'm the boss."

Gregory Olsen, who had watched the encounter from his machine-gun position a few dozen meters away, said that "the next thing I knew Mitchell was just shooting into the ditch." At this point Grzesik and his fire team came strolling into the area; they had gone completely through the hamlet, had a break, and were now returning. It was about ten o'-clock. Grzesik saw bodies all over the northeastern quarter of My Lai 4. He glanced at the ditch. Suddenly Mitchell yelled, "Grzesik, come here." He walked over. Calley then ordered him to go to the ditch and "finish off the people." Grzesik had seen the helicopter carrying some wounded

Vietnamese take off from the area a moment earlier; much later he concluded that Calley—furious with Thompson's intervention—wanted to make sure there were no more survivors in the ditch. Calley told Grzesik to gather his team to do the job. "I really believe he expected me to do it," Grzesik said later, with some amazement. Calley asked him again, and Grzesik again refused. The lieutenant then angrily ordered him to take his team and help burn the hootches. Grzesik headed for the hamlet plaza.

Thompson continued to fly over the ditch and noticed that some of the children's bodies had no heads. He landed a third time after his crew chief told him that he had seen some movement in the mass of bodies and blood below. The crew chief and Colburn began walking toward the ditch. "Nobody said anything," Colburn said. "We just got out." They found a young child still alive. No GIs were in the immediate area, but Colburn was carrying a rifle. The crew chief climbed into the ditch. "He was knee-deep in people and blood," Colburn recalled. The child was quiet, buried under many bodies. "He was still holding onto his mother. But she was dead." The boy, clinging desperately, was pried loose. He still did not cry. Thompson later told the IG, "I don't think this child was even wounded at all, just down there among all the other bodies, and he was terrified." Thompson and his men flew the baby to safety.

In other parts of My Lai 4, GIs were taking a break, or loafing. Others were systematically burning those remaining houses and huts and destroying food. Some villagers—still alive—were able to leave their hiding places and walk away. Charles West recalled that one member of his squad who simply wasn't able to slaughter a group of children asked for and received permission from an officer to let them go. West's third platoon went ahead, nonetheless, with the killing. They gathered a group of about ten women and children, who huddled together in fear a few feet from the plaza, where dozens of villagers already had been slain. West and the squad had finished their mission in the north and west of the hamlet, and were looking for new targets. They drifted south toward the CP. Jay Roberts and Ron Haeberle, who had spent the past hour watching the slaughter in other parts of the hamlet, stood by—pencil and cameras at the ready. A few men now singled out a slender Vietnamese girl of about fifteen. They tore her from the group and started to pull at her blouse. They attempted to fondle her breasts. The old women and children were screaming and crying. One GI yelled, "Let's see what she's made of." Another said, "VC Boom, Boom," meaning she was a Viet Cong whore. Jay Roberts thought that the girl was good-looking. An old lady began fighting with fanatical fury, trying to protect the girl. Roberts said, "She was fighting off two or three guys at once. She was fantastic. Usually they're pretty passive . . . They hadn't even gotten that chick's blouse off when Haeberle came along." One of the GIs finally smacked the old woman with his rifle butt; another booted her in the rear.

Grzesik and his fire team watched the fight develop as they walked down from the ditch to the hamlet center. Grzesik was surprised: "I thought the village was cleared . . . I didn't know there were that many people left." He knew trouble was brewing, and his main thought was to keep his team out of it. He helped break up the fight. Some of the children were desperately hanging onto the old lady as she struggled. Grzesik was worried about the cameraman. He may have yelled, "Hey, there's a photographer." He remembered thinking, "Here's a guy standing there with a camera that you've never seen before." Then somebody said, "What do we do with them?" The answer was, "Waste them." Suddenly there was a burst of automatic fire from many guns. Only a small child survived. Somebody then carefully shot him, too. A photograph of the woman and child, with the young Vietnamese girl tucking in her blouse, was later published in *Life* magazine. Roberts tried to explain later: "It's just that they didn't know what they were supposed to do; killing them seemed like a good idea, so they did it. The old lady who fought so hard was probably a VC." He thought a moment and added, "Maybe it was just her daughter."

West was annoyed at the photographer: "I thought it was wrong for him to stand up and take pictures of this thing. Even though we had to do it, I thought, we didn't have to take pictures of it." Later he complained personally to Haeberle about it.

By now it was nearly 10:30 A.M. and most of the company began drifting aimlessly toward the plaza and the command post a few yards to the south. Their work was largely over; a good part of the hamlet was in flames. The villagers "were laying around like ants," William Wyatt remembered. "It was just like somebody had poisoned the water and everybody took a drink and started falling out."

Herb Carter and Harry Stanley had shed their gear and were taking a short break at the CP. Near them was a young Vietnamese boy, crying, with a bullet wound in his stomach. Stanley watched one of Captain Medina's three radio operators walk along a trail toward them; he was without his radio gear. As Stanley told the C.I.D., the radio operator went up to Carter and said, "Let me see your pistol." Carter gave it to him. The radio operator "then stepped within two feet of the boy and shot him in the neck with a pistol. Blood gushed from the child's neck. He then tried to walk off, but he could only take two or three steps. Then he fell onto the ground. He lay there and took four or five deep breaths and then he stopped breathing." The radio operator turned to Stanley and said, "Did you see how I shot that son of a bitch?" Stanley told him, "I don't see how anyone could just kill a kid." Carter got his pistol back; he told Stanley, "I can't take this no more . . ." Moments later Stanley heard a gun go off and Carter yell. "I went to Carter and saw he had shot himself in the foot. I think Carter shot himself on purpose."

Other children were also last-minute targets. After the scene with the women and children, West noticed a small boy, about seven years old, staring dazedly beside a footpath. He had been shot in the leg. "He was just standing there staring; I don't think he was crying. Somebody asked, 'What do we do with him?' " At this point West had remembered there had been an order from Captain Medina to stop the shooting. "I just shrugged my shoulders," West recalled, "and said, 'I don't know,' and just kept walking." Seconds later he heard some shots, turned around and saw the boy no longer standing on the trail.

Haeberle and Roberts were walking together on the edge of the hamlet when they also noticed the wounded child with the vacant stare. In seconds, Roberts said, "Haeberle, envisioning the war-torn-wounded-waif picture of the year, got within five feet of the kid for a close-up. He was focusing when some guy, just walking along, leveled his rifle, fired three times and walked away." Haeberle saw the shooting through the lens of his camera. "He looked up in shock," Roberts added. "He just turned around and stared. I think that was the thing that stayed in our mind. It was so close, so real, we just saw some kid blown away."

By then a helicopter, called in by Medina, had landed near the command post to fly out the wounded Carter. Sergeant Duong Minh, the interpreter who had angered Medina with his questions about the dead civilians, was also put aboard.

One of Haeberle's photographs shows the company medic, Nicholas Capezza of Queens, New York, bandaging Carter, with Medina and a radio operator, Rodger Murray of Waukegan, Illinois, in the background near a partially destroyed red-brick house. Medina was on the radio. William Wyatt remembered the scene; that was the first time he'd seen Medina that morning. Roy Wood also saw him then for the first time. Others recalled, however, that the captain had left his CP south of the plaza many times during the late morning to tour the northern and western sections, urging the men to stop the shooting and get on with the job of burning down the buildings. Some GIs from the second platoon, under Lieutenant Brooks, found three men still alive. Gary Crossley heard the GIs ask Brooks, "What do we do now?" The lieutenant relayed the question by radio to Medina. "Don't kill them," the captain said. "There's been too much of that already." Gary Garfolo remembered that Medina seemed frantic at times, literally dashing about the hamlet. "He was telling everybody, 'Let's start getting out—let's move out of here.' "

Roberts also thought that Medina "was all over." He and Haeberle had crossed from the south to the north side of the hamlet to look around, and saw the captain there. "Then Carter shot himself and Medina went back," Roberts said. At some point earlier in the morning, Roberts had watched some GIs interrogate an old man. He didn't know anything, and somebody asked the captain what to do with him. Medina "indicated he didn't care," Roberts said, "that the guy wasn't of any use to him, and walked away." The GIs shot the man. Sergeant Mitchell may have witnessed the same scene. He saw both Calley and Medina interrogating an old man; Mitchell thought he was a monk. "Four or five of us weren't far away. We were watching. The old monk mumbled something and Medina walked off. I looked away for a second, and when I looked back the old man had been shot and Calley was standing over him."

Richard Pendleton remembered Medina himself shooting a civilian that day. Pendleton was standing about fifty feet away from the captain sometime that morning—Pendleton isn't sure exactly when. Pendleton hadn't seen the captain earlier and he wondered what Medina thought about what was going on. "Medina was standing there with the rest of the CP. It was right there in the open. I was watching." There was a small Vietnamese child, "the only one alive among a lot of dead people." He said he watched Medina carefully aim his M16 rifle at the child. "He shot him in the head, and he went down."

Pendleton may have been mistaken. There was a child shot near the command post that day, after Carter shot himself. Charles Gruver of Tulsa, Oklahoma, remembered vividly how it happened: he saw a small boy, about three or four years old, standing by a trail with a wound in his arm. "He just stood there with big eyes staring like he didn't believe what was happening. Then the captain's RTO [radio operator] put a burst of 16 [M16 rifle fire] into him." Ronald Grzesik also saw it. He was just watching the child when he heard a rifle shot; he looked back and saw that the radio operator was still in braced firing position. But Medina, Grzesik recalled, "was around the corner" in the command post at the time. Roberts also witnessed the shooting; he thought the toddler was searching through the pile of dead bodies for his mother or father, or a sister. He was wearing only a shirt. The impact of the M16 flung the small body backward onto the pile.

After that incident Grzesik said he went up to John Paul, one of Medina's radiomen, and told him what had been go-

ing on inside My Lai 4. Paul promptly asked him to tell the
captain. Grzesik declined, thinking that Medina "was going
to find out anyway if he walked up a few feet."

There were some small acts of mercy. A GI placed a
blanket over the body of a mutilated child. An elderly
woman was spared when some GIs hollered at a soldier just
as he was about to shoot her. Grzesik remembered watching
a GI seem to wrestle with his conscience while holding a
bayonet over a wounded old man. "He wants to stab somebody with a bayonet," Grzesik thought. The GI hesitated
. . . and finally passed on, leaving the old man to die.

Some GIs, however, didn't hesitate to use their bayonets.
Nineteen-year-old Nguyen Thi Ngoc Tuyet watched a baby
trying to open her slain mother's blouse to nurse. A soldier
shot the infant while it was struggling with the blouse, and
then slashed at it with his bayonet. Tuyet also said she saw
another baby hacked to death by GIs wielding their bayonets.

Le Tong, a twenty-eight-year-old rice farmer, reported
seeing one woman raped after GIs killed her children. Nguyen Khoa, a thirty-seven-year-old peasant, told of a thirteen-
year-old girl who was raped before being killed. GIs then attacked Khoa's wife, tearing off her clothes. Before they could
rape her, however, Khoa said, their six-year-old son, riddled
with bullets, fell and saturated her with blood. The GIs left
her alone.

There were "degrees" of murder that day. Some were conducted out of sympathy. Michael Terry, the Mormon who
was a squad leader in the third platoon, had ordered his men
to take their lunch break by the bloody ditch in the rear of
the hamlet. He noticed that there were no men in the ditch,
only women and children. He had watched Calley and the
others shoot into that ditch. Calley seemed just like a kid,
Terry thought. He also remembered thinking it was "just

like a Nazi-type thing." When one soldier couldn't fire any more and threw down his weapon, "Calley picked it up." Later, during lunch, Terry and his men saw that some of the victims were still breathing. "They were pretty badly shot up. They weren't going to get any medical help, and so we shot them. Shot maybe five of them."

James Bergthold saw an old man who had been shot in both legs: "He was going to die anyway, so I figured I might as well kill him." He took his .45-caliber pistol (as a machine-gun ammunition carrier, he was entitled to one), carefully placed the barrel against the upper part of the old man's forehead and blew off the top of his head. Carter had watched the scene and remembered thinking that Bergthold had done the old man a favor. "If me and you were together and you got wounded bad," Carter later told an interviewer, "and I couldn't get you to a doctor, I'd shoot you, too."

Most of the shooting was over by the time Medina called a break for lunch, shortly after eleven o'clock. By then Roberts and Haeberle had grabbed a helicopter and cleared out of the area, their story for the day far bigger than they wanted. Calley, Mitchell, Sledge, Grzesik and a few others went back to the command post west of My Lai 4 to take lunch with Captain Medina and the rest of his headquarter's crew. Grzesik recalled that at that point he'd thought there couldn't be a survivor left in the hamlet. But two little girls showed up, about ten and eleven years old. John Paul said they came in from one of the paddies, where they apparently had waited out the siege. "We sat them down with us [at the command post]," Paul recounted, "and gave them some cookies and crackers to eat." When a C.I.D. interrogator later asked Charles Sledge how many civilians he thought had survived, he answered, "Only two small children who had lunch with us."

In the early afternoon the men of Charlie Company mopped up to make sure all the houses and goods in My Lai 4 were destroyed. Medina ordered the underground tunnels in the hamlet blown up; most of them already had been blocked. Within another hour My Lai 4 was no more: its red-brick buildings demolished by explosives, its huts burned to the ground, its people dead or dying.

Michael Bernhardt later summarized the day: "We met no resistance and I only saw three captured weapons. We had no casualties. It was just like any other Vietnamese village—old papa-sans, women and kids. As a matter of fact, I don't remember seeing one military-age male in the entire place, dead or alive. The only prisoner I saw was in his fifties."

The platoons pulled out shortly after noon, rendezvousing in the rice paddies east of My Lai 4. Lieutenant Brooks' platoon had about eighty-five villagers in tow; it kept those of military age with them and told the rest to begin moving south. Following orders, Medina then marched the GIs northeast through the nearly deserted hamlets of My Lai 5 and My Lai 6, ransacking and burning as they went. In one of the hamlets, Medina ordered the residents gathered, and then told Sergeant Phu, the regular company interpreter, to tell them, as Phu later recalled, that "they were to go away or something will happen to them—just like what happened at My Lai 4."

By nightfall the Viet Cong were back in My Lai 4, helping the survivors bury the dead. It took five days. Most of the funeral speeches were made by the Communist guerrillas. Nguyen Bat was not a Communist at the time of the massacre, but the incident changed his mind. "After the shooting," he said, "all the villagers became Communists."

When Army investigators reached the barren area in November, 1969, in connection with the My Lai probe in the United States, they found mass graves at three sites, as well as a ditch full of bodies. It was estimated that between 450 and 500 people—most of them women, children and old men—had been slain and buried there.

5

Victory

SPECIALIST 5 Jay Roberts carried his reporter's notepad and a pencil with him when he took the helicopter from 11th Brigade headquarters at Duc Pho early that morning. But whatever he wrote could not be used. The Army had decided the night before that the Viet Cong were in My Lai 4; nothing that happened in the next twenty-four hours officially changed that view.

A Saigon report of Charlie Company's battle sent to the Pentagon the night of March 16 noted that initial "contact with the enemy force" occurred at 7:50 A.M., about the time Lieutenant Calley and his platoon had secured the landing zone and shot an unarmed old man. The military message added that a second combat company had been airlifted into the area by 9:10 A.M. and that both units reported "sporadic contact" with the enemy as they moved toward a rendezvous. The companies had support from "Army artillery and helicopter gunships."

Roberts—who had been out of My Lai 4 since 11 A.M.—learned from Colonel Barker in the early afternoon that the final body count for Task Force Barker that day was 128, with three enemy weapons captured. He had no idea how, or why, that total was reached. There was great excitement at LZ Dotti: the 128 body count was the largest for the Task Force since it had begun operations forty days earlier. The correspondent knew most of the dead were civilians; he personally had seen at least twenty-five persons killed and fifty bodies: "I was pretty upset. And then I had to write a story about it. How do you write a story when you have 128 bodies and only three captured weapons?" He thought briefly of reporting what had happened, but decided against it when he walked into the Tactical Operations Center at LZ Dotti. He was promptly kicked out of the area by Major Charles Calhoun, the Task Force operations officer who was monitoring the radios. Roberts still doesn't know if he was thrown out because of what was coming over the radios or because of simple officer hostility to enlisted men. In either case, the incident didn't bolster his courage. Colonel Barker also returned to his headquarters at Duc Pho early in the afternoon, and Roberts sought him out. Roberts asked him "about the high body count and the low number of weapons discovered. He just kind of overlooked it and said something to the effect that I could make a good story without that fact." Barker died in a helicopter crash three months later, but Roberts was certain "he knew what was going on. He knew they were wiping out the village." The correspondent returned to headquarters at Duc Pho.

Roberts wrote the story based on the official statistics and gave it to his superior officer. "I just figured it'd look real bad, and it wasn't my problem." The brigade press officer, Second Lieutenant Arthur Dunn of Forest Park, Illinois, also thought the story looked bad. Dunn particularly noticed the claim that high numbers of Viet Cong were killed and the fact that artillery had been called in before the ground assault. "Well, they did it again," he said to himself, thinking that an artillery round had landed amidst civilians. Dunn's job was to file a daily after-action report on the brigade's maneuvers to division headquarters at Chu Lai. Task Force Barker's assault on My Lai 4 was the biggest thing going on March 16, and Dunn used the same official statistics that were available to Roberts. As he wrote his report that evening he knew it "was fishy." Perhaps, he thought, Medina and his company had unearthed some previously killed soldiers or civilians and were claiming them as enemy dead. Such things had happened before.

Roberts hadn't discussed the mission with him, Dunn recalled, but it wouldn't have made any difference if he had: "If I had known there was a massacre and let somebody write about it, I would have lost my job." The young officer's two-page action report was dictated that night by telephone to the American Division press office at Chu Lai. "They copied it down word for word," Dunn said. Division press personnel sent one copy of the story up to Saigon for release to the hundreds of newsmen there; a second copy was sent over to the printer for publication in the division's daily newsletter. The report bore little relation to reality. Neither did Roberts'.

The official brigade account of the Task Force operation, as written by Roberts, gave Charlie Company direct credit for only fifteen of the 128 enemy kills, and also said that none of the company's victims was inside My Lai 4 at the time. "The infantry company led by Captain Ernest Medina engaged and killed fourteen VC and captured three M-1 rifles, a radio and enemy documents while moving toward the village," the report said, adding that one Vietnamese had been killed earlier at the landing zone. It said firefights in the surrounding areas were responsible for most of the enemy deaths. Six victims were killed by the helicopter gunships from the 123rd Aviation Battalion and 174th Aviation Company, which were flying support for the mission. Those six, according to Roberts' version, were the only Vietnamese who were killed inside My Lai 4. Barker was quoted in the story as saying, "The combat assault went like clockwork. We had two entire companies on the ground in less than an hour." The story added that "the swiftness with which the units moved into the area surprised the enemy. After the battle, the 11th Brigade soldiers moved into the village, searching each hut and tunnel."

Similar stories appeared later in the *Pacific Stars and Stripes* and in the *Trident,* the weekly newspaper of the Americal Division.

A report of the My Lai 4 invasion, based on the official version supplied newsmen in Saigon, was published on the front page of *The New York Times,* as well as in many other newspapers, on March 17. It said that two Americal Division companies had caught a North Vietnamese unit in a pincer movement, killing 128 enemy soldiers. "The United States soldiers were sweeping the area . . . " the *Times* said. "The operation is another American offensive to clear enemy pockets still threatening the cities. While the two companies of United States soldiers moved in on the enemy force from opposite sides, heavy artillery barrages and armed helicopters were called in to pound the North Vietnamese soldiers." The report said two American GIs were killed and ten wounded during the day-long fight six miles northeast of Quang Ngai, even though Medina's company had sustained only one casualty—Carter. There was no mention of civilian casualties.

Haeberle had returned with Roberts to Duc Pho. He

developed some—but not all—of the photographs taken at My Lai 4 that day. He had taken three cameras with him; one to shoot black-and-white photographs for the Army and two to shoot color photographs for his own use. A few black-and-white photographs were printed and sent up to division headquarters, but only a few. Most of the negatives were simply thrown into a desk at Duc Pho. Roberts obviously thought that there was no sense in sending up photographs of carnage, because the press people at headquarters would never have approved them for release.

Charlie Company's apparent victory did not go unnoticed. A few days after the battle, General William C. Westmoreland, then commander of U. S. forces in Vietnam, sent the following message: "Operation Muscatine [the code name for the My Lai 4 assault] contact northeast of Quang Ngai City on 16 March dealt enemy heavy blow. Congratulations to officers and men of C-1-20 [Charlie Company, 1st Battalion, 20th Infantry] for outstanding action."

6

Aftermath

*H*OURS after it was over, most members of Charlie Company were still keyed up. There was a lot of talk, much of it bragging about how many gooks had been killed that day. Harry Stanley said that three members of the company had staged a contest at My Lai 4 to see who would kill the most people there. Charles West got angry at all the loose talk and joking after the incident: "It was bad enough that we did this, but some guys were telling how many people they had killed . . . this didn't make no sense. The guys wasn't unhappy until after we came out; until they stopped to think about what they did."

When the men of Charlie Company finished razing My Lai 5 and 6, Medina marched them south to meet up with another company of Task Force Barker; together the units would set up defensive positions for the night near the South China Sea coast a few miles to the east. By late afternoon the

company was about 2,500 meters—well over a mile—outside the hamlet. Medina got a radio call from Major Calhoun, asking him to take the company back into My Lai 4
to do a better body count of civilian casualties. Medina
argued: "I said I felt that was too far to go and it was late
in the day and that it would be better to go into defensive
positions." He was afraid of mines and booby traps: "This
was a very dangerous operation in dangerous territory."

Suddenly General Koster, apparently flying overhead in
a helicopter and monitoring the conversation between
Medina and Calhoun, broke in over the radio, using his
code name "Saber Six." Medina recalled that "Saber Six
said there was no need to send the company . . . back into
all that mess" this late in the day. Saber Six asked how many
civilians had been killed during the operation in My Lai 4.
Medina told him "about twenty to twenty-eight." Koster
replied, "That sounds about right," and ordered Medina to
get his defensive positions set up for the night. At some
point that evening Medina gathered his three platoon
leaders and asked if any civilians had been killed. "I received negative indications," he recalled.

Later that night Medina told his men that a helicopter
pilot had filed a complaint and there was the possibility of
an investigation. Bernhardt remembered Medina's promising
that he would back them up in case of trouble: "He said he
would say that there was a gunfight and that we did a lot
of shooting." The captain urged his men not to talk about
it. "The guys weren't worried," Bernhardt added. "They had
absolute faith in him."

Charlie Company heard no more officially about My Lai
4 that day. But they talked among themselves. Mike Terry
shared his dinner that night with Gregory Olsen and Michael
Bernhardt. They were all upset about what had happened.

"We talked about the way the Army was going to cover it by saying it was such a good thing . . . a big victory," Terry recalled. All three thought that field grade officers must have known about it. Bernhardt heard talk of a body count of "over three hundred" in My Lai; he also heard that only those old enough to walk were tallied. Young children and infants were not. Paul Meadlo was deeply disturbed about what he had done, especially after someone told him that the company was not supposed to kill everybody: "Mitchell said we were just supposed to shoot the men." James Bergthold remembered "everybody was talking about it. First we heard there were quite a lot killed and then it was found out they weren't supposed to be killed, but were supposed to have been evacuated by helicopters instead."

They didn't dwell on it too long, however. John Paul remembered that some of the GIs brought two girls—apparently taken from one of the My Lai hamlets—down to the beach. He isn't sure what happened to them.

At one point in the evening a GI approached Sergeant Phu, who was distressed by what had happened to his countrymen that day, and suggested that he try not to look so unhappy because "it could be very dangerous" for him. He was told to "look casual."

Back at Duc Pho, Captain Charlie R. Lewellen, assistant intelligence officer for Task Force Barker, was just getting to sleep after an exhausting day. He liked to tape radio transmissions during combat: "It's one thing to tell a man what combat's like, it's another to play a tape." He had set up his equipment at the communications center at Duc Pho early in the morning. The first words recorded, he said later, showed that the "lift ships were getting off the ground at 7:22 A.M." The tape played continuously during the day, transcribing all of the complaints made by Thompson and the transmission between Medina and others in the 11th Brigade. Lewellen kept the Japanese-made recorder going until "I checked out and went to bed."

Charlie Company spent that night in a Vietnamese grave-yard, their sleeping bags and pup tents flung amidst shrines and burial mounds.

The next morning Medina was ordered by Task Force Barker to establish an outpost on a nearby hill and destroy three deserted hamlets named Mykhe 1, 2 and 3. Sometime that day there was another argument in the first platoon be-tween Calley and Sergeant Cowen, and another casualty resulted. The mission was reconnaissance; Calley wanted to take a small squad to the top of a ridge that was marked off limits on the map because of minefields. Cowen argued briefly, but gave up when Calley asked his usual question: "Who's the boss?" The lieutenant picked Meadlo and a few others to go along. Meadlo had the minesweeper that day: his job was to go before the others and carefully sweep the warning device back and forth a few inches off the ground. His mind was on other things; he got careless and triggered a mine that blew off his right foot. Charles Sledge heard Meadlo begin to yell and curse at Calley while waiting for a rescue helicopter, warning him that "God will punish you. If you don't get out of the field, the same thing will happen to you." Rennard Doines also heard Meadlo say to Calley, "God will punish you for what you made me do." Some of the mine fragments had struck Calley and slightly wounded him about the face—he got a Purple Heart for the injury. Calley was shaken. He began screaming, "Get him on the helicopter. Get him on the helicopter." Describing the inci-dent twenty months later, Wood commented that "maybe God done caught up with Calley. It seems to me that now he got his reward, too."

During the search-and-destroy missions, some GIs seemed to get out of control again. Three men and a woman were sighted fleeing from a burning hut in one of the hamlets. The woman was grabbed. Gregory Olsen saw a soldier from the second platoon running around with the woman, by this time stripped of all her clothing, over his shoulder. "He said he was going to 'put it' to her, but she was too dirty," Olsen recalled. The men were all told that the woman had been identified as a North Vietnamese army nurse; the men with her, who had escaped, were described as doctors. Roy Wood remembered clearly that they didn't get the men, but the whole second platoon got her—"they caught her ass." Wood said, "They all raped her . . . tore her up." He saw her later, bleeding badly, but one of the sergeants fixed her up. Later she escaped. "Tough?" he asked rhetorically. "She sure must of been—she took on all of them." The incident, which took place hardly twenty-four hours after the assault on My Lai 4, was known to most members of the company.

Charlie Company eventually worked its way back to the South China Sea coast, where four suspects were captured, including a young boy and a middle-aged man. The boy was gagged and tied to a bamboo tree; he quickly identified the man as an area commander for the North Vietnamese army. The men decided to have some fun. One GI lit a cigarette and stuffed it, still burning, inside the older man's pants. Grzesik watched as the man started to dance in pain and the GI danced alongside, mocking him. John Kinch said that Medina played Russian roulette with the man at one point, trying futilely to make him talk. "Then he grabbed him by the hair and threw him up against a tree. He fired two shots with a rifle, closer and closer to the guy's head, and then aimed straight at him." The captive began talking. He said he was a North Vietnamese army area commander. Medina later had a photograph taken of himself drinking from a coconut with one hand and holding a sharp knife under the throat of the trussed-up boy.

Sometime in the afternoon of that day, March 17, Medina got a call from Task Force Barker headquarters informing him that Colonel Henderson, the brigade commander, was en route for a visit. The colonel, accompanied by two other officers, landed and told Medina he had been accused of shooting a woman at My Lai 4. The colonel said he was conducting an informal investigation. "He asked me if there had been any war crimes at My Lai 4, and I told him no," Medina recalled. Henderson left. By this time word of Charlie Company's victory at My Lai 4 was on the front page of *The New York Times* and General Westmoreland's office was readying his routine message of congratulations.

But Medina was worried. John Smail of Renton, Washington, a squad leader in the third platoon, remembered thinking that "somebody gave him a good ass-chewing." Smail and Medina got along well; the GI said that "Medina liked to bullshit with me, but he just wasn't himself" after Henderson's visit. "He was sweating about something," Smail said. "He walked around real nervously, and kept on saying, 'Sergeant Smail, what can I do?' I asked him, 'What do you mean, sir?'"

The next day Charlie Company returned to LZ Dotti, its mission a success. As they climbed off the helicopters onto the landing pad, some of the men were quizzed by Colonel Henderson about My Lai 4, but all denied seeing indiscriminate shooting. For most of the GIs, that was the last they would hear about My Lai 4 from their officers or brigade headquarters.

Michael Bernhardt, however, wanted to do something about what he had seen. But he was afraid to speak out. He had watched as Colonel Henderson queried the men, and he felt sure nothing would come of it. He thought, too, that the helicopter pilot who had reported the incident had been killed in action the next day. Not many could speak, he figured, without implicating themselves, and if they did, no one knew how the Army would react. Bernhardt felt he had no place to go. He decided he could, perhaps, write his congressman about the shooting. He apparently mentioned his idea to other members of his platoon; the word got to the platoon leader, Lieutenant Stephen Brooks. Brooks passed it on to Medina. The captain accosted Bernhardt in a mess hall, and told the rifleman, "You can write your congressman if you want to. But you will create a big stink. The matter is being investigated." Medina did not spell out just what could be reported to the congressman, but it was clear to both men what they were talking about. Bernhardt denied that he had any such plan; Medina then emphasized that it would be unwise to send such a letter. An Army investigation concluded more than a year later that Medina had not really threatened the youth; he had merely "encouraged" him not to write any letters.

A few days after Charlie Company's invasion of My Lai 4, Ronald L. Ridenhour, a GI from Phoenix, Arizona, then serving as a helicopter door gunner in the 11th Brigade, flew over the stricken area: "The hamlet was completely desolate. There were no people around, no signs of life anywhere." The pilot, Warrant Officer Gilbert Honda, hovered the craft over a rice paddy near the hamlet. Ridenhour saw a body below. The helicopter flew down to investigate. "It was a woman," Ridenhour remembered, "spread-eagled as if on display. She had an 11th Brigade patch between her legs—as if it were some type of display, some badge of honor. We just looked; it was obviously there so people would know the 11th Brigade had been there. We just thought, 'What in the hell's wrong with these guys? What's going on?' "

The pilot banked the helicopter so its prop wash caught the patch and blew it away. Moments later Ridenhour spotted a number of possible Viet Cong suspects walking together in the My Lai 4 area. The men ran and jumped into a bunker when the helicopter approached. Ridenhour wanted to flush them out with a white phosphorous grenade to determine if they were Viet Cong. "They were obviously bad guys," he recalled. But Honda seemed reluctant, and half-heartedly flew the helicopter over the bunker—at far too high an altitude to hit it with a grenade. Ridenhour was angry: "What in hell's going on, sir?" Honda told him cryptically that "these people around here have had a pretty rough time the last few days." The helicopter flew off.

Within hours, word of what had happened in My Lai 4 had spread throughout the helicopter units of the 11th Brigade. "We just rapped about it," Larry Colburn recalled. "Guys in the 123rd Aviation saw it and got mad. Thompson was so pissed he wanted to turn in his wings."

Charlie Company quickly settled back into its routine of search-and-destroy missions, which continued until its year in Vietnam was over. There were only a few reminders of what had happened. Somehow other companies in the 1st Battalion of the 11th Brigade had learned about My Lai 4. "They'd say, 'Yeah, we heard you killed a whole lot of women and children—and then reported 128 VC killed,' " West recalled. Charles Sledge also remembered, with unhappiness, the fact that other companies "would razz us about it."

Medina promoted Calley to first lieutenant soon after My Lai, but his platoon continued in its dislike and disrespect for its young officer. In April, 1968, the long-simmering feud between Sergeant Cowen and Lieutenant Calley reached its climax when Calley insisted during a field operation that artillery be called in near the first platoon's position. Cowen demanded he cancel the order. Calley refused. "I told him that someday he'd be sorry he never listened to a noncom," Cowen recalled. "I grabbed Mitchell and told him we'd better find a hole and crawl in it . . . We were sitting there talking when I heard the whistle of an incoming. It landed fifty meters away. I could hear Calley yelling on the phone for the artillery to stop. The next night we hooked with the company again and I had a talk with Medina. I told him, 'It's either Calley or me.' "

The following day Calley was relieved and put in charge of the mortar platoon, whose responsibility was to provide artillery cover for the infantrymen in the company. John Paul said that Medina must have made the shift after "figuring out where Calley could do the least damage." Calley later requested a transfer out of Charlie Company—and got it.

By then Medina's men were talking much less about My Lai 4. If there was any general consensus among the members of Charlie Company, it was perhaps best expressed by William Doherty, who thought "it was pretty disgusting, but it was a different feeling. If they had been Americans," he said of the dead Vietnamese, "I might have felt different. I never really understood those people." Doherty was upset by what had happened to him in Vietnam: "You'd see a guy's leg blown off, or a rifle wound through his head—it stopped meaning anything more. It was nothing. You'd just say, 'Glad it wasn't me.' They told me this would happen to me when I got to Nam—this attitude. I didn't believe it, but . . ."

No one had stepped forward in protest, and most of the

men started brooding about the incident only after they left the company or returned to their homes in the United States. Larry Colburn later bumped into some GIs at Fort Hood, Texas, who had served in other units of Task Force Barker at the time of My Lai 4. He talked to them about it. "They heard that Charlie Company had a turkey shoot," Colburn recalled.

At least one GI, however, had second thoughts while still with Medina's company in Vietnam. Ron Grzesik said that he wasn't immediately distressed by what he saw that day; four days after My Lai 4 he wrote a friend back home without even mentioning the shootings. But the following week he sent another letter, this one describing what had happened and concluding that every man in Charlie Company "should be sent to jail."

7

The Cover-Up

*T*HE Army defines the shooting of unarmed civilians as a "grave breach" of the Geneva Convention of August 12, 1949, for the protection of war victims. A 1968 directive published by the United States command in Saigon is explicit about what to do: "It is the responsibility of all military personnel having knowledge or receiving a report of an incident or of an act thought to be a war crime to make such incident known to his commanding officer as soon as possible. . . . Persons discovering war crimes will take all reasonable action under the circumstances to preserve physical evidence, to note identity of witnesses present, and to record the circumstances and surroundings." In addition, the directive requires that all such information should be made known "as soon as practical" to officials in the Saigon command.

March 16, 1968, was Colonel Oran Henderson's first day on his new job. He had been promoted from executive officer to commanding officer of the 11th Brigade during ceremonies twenty-four hours earlier at Duc Pho, relieving Brigadier General Andy A. Lipscomb.

It should have been a happy day. But things began going wrong for Henderson right from the start. Shortly after nine that morning the colonel, cruising above the battle in My Lai 4, noticed two men fleeing the hamlet. He thought they might be Viet Cong, and ordered Warrant Officer Thompson, below him in a small observation helicopter, to stop them. After this was done, Henderson landed and personally interrogated the suspects. They turned out to be, Thompson later told the Inspector General, not Viet Cong but two members of the Saigon government's local militia, who had apparently been held captive in My Lai 4.

Sometime in that same hour Thompson filed his complaint to brigade headquarters about the "wild shooting by men on the ground and by helicopters in the area." He specifically cited the shooting of a woman by an army captain. Upon learning of the complaint, Henderson said later, "I reported it to division headquarters [at Chu Lai] right away." He told them that he would make an inquiry. Henderson already had had some hints of wild shooting at My Lai 4 before he heard from Thompson. In the fall of 1969 Henderson told a reporter that on an earlier helicopter fly-by, he had seen the bodies of "five or six" civilians, two of which appeared to be men. He said nothing then; after all, he explained, "I know that sometimes civilians get killed accidentally in war."

But the colonel, testifying in the spring of '69 in private at the Pentagon about the incident, had had a different recollection: he had observed the bodies of only one woman and two children, both killed—he believed—by artillery. The Army subsequently asked Thompson about that statement, and the warrant officer—who had landed his helicopter in the same area at the same time—disagreed. "There was more," Thompson testified in June, 1969. "I would say on this stretch of road there was eight or ten [bodies] and that is probably putting it mildly because there were probably that many buffalo or oxen."

Henderson gave a third version of what he saw. He told a group of radio and television newsmen in November, 1969, that he had flown over My Lai 4 and had seen no evidence of a massacre. By the end of the next day, March 17, Henderson said, he had questioned the men of Charlie Company and they proclaimed their innocence.

There is yet another version of Henderson's involvement. Larry Colburn decided to tell somebody what he had witnessed in My Lai 4. After returning in the afternoon to brigade headquarters at Duc Pho, he walked over to Henderson's office. "I told him what happened that day," Colburn said. "He took a few notes and then I just never heard anything about it." The colonel seemed "nonchalant" about the whole affair. Colburn wasn't surprised: "I never thought anything would come of it anyway. I'd seen it happen before, but just not with that many people." Thompson accompanied his young crew member to the colonel's quarters. Colburn recalled that the pilot also spoke to Henderson that day.

This was only the beginning of many contradictions in the subsequent accounts by Henderson and others of how the colonel learned about and investigated the charges of wild shooting and unnecessary killing in My Lai 4.

Lieutenant Colonel Barker, the Task Force commander, and Major Charles Calhoun, its executive officer at LZ Dotti, were immediately informed of Thompson's complaint. It is not known if anyone else immediately knew of it. Barker contacted Medina, who then radioed Calley to ask what was going on and to tell him to conserve ammunition. All of these messages were being carefully logged on Lewellen's tape recorder at the communications center at Duc Pho. Second Lieutenant Joseph Reid, of Mountain View, California, was monitoring the radios at brigade headquarters at Duc Pho that day; he heard radio messages indicating that "the going was pretty thick."

Thompson's report could not be ignored. Army Secretary Stanley R. Resor later said that Henderson was immediately "directed to conduct an investigation of the incident." It is unclear who actually gave Henderson the order. The colonel, in his subsequent description of his actions to newsmen, indicated that he himself had initiated the brief field investigation on March 17, and went on to say that he had interrogated a suspect that day in connection with a shooting at My Lai 4. In his first public discussions of the case, however, Henderson did not identify Medina as the man who was being investigated for the murder, nor did he say the victim was a woman.

Henderson's version of the shooting of the woman was similar in all aspects to that given the IG by Thompson and Colburn, with this important exception: "The individual [Medina] thought this [Vietnamese] person was dead, and as he walked away, the Vietnamese raised his arm, and instinctively the individual thought it was a hand grenade. He whipped out and fired with his weapon, and it was a regrettable incident. But as a soldier, I can accept this. It was purely a result of the survival problem you're faced with. You only have a split second to react." The on-the-spot interrogations in connection with the shooting of the woman were ended at that point, apparently because of Medina's explanation.

Henderson also gave two accounts of his subsequent interrogation on March 18 of some of the men of Charlie Company at LZ Dotti. He told one reporter: "I talked to about forty of them and I asked them point-blank if there was any truth to these reports. This was an informal inquiry. I got a negative from all of them. In all my questioning, there was only one admission that a civilian had been killed . . . [a reference to the Medina shooting]." According to another newspaper version supplied by Henderson, he gathered thirty or forty men, and approximately the following happened:

"From initial reports he [Henderson] had, some civilians might have been killed, perhaps promiscuously. This overshadowed to a degree any success they had in the operation. It concerned him as brigade commander. He did not expect his soldiers to kill civilians. He asked whether anyone in the group had observed shooting or killing of civilians. Reportedly there was a general murmur: 'No, no.' He pointed his finger at random at three or four men, and asked each of them. 'No, sir,' came the answer, loud and clear."

One of the men he asked was Sergeant Cowen. "When we got out of the area," Cowen recalled, "some colonel came up and asked me if there was anything unusual going on in the village. I said, 'No comment,' and he passed on." Allen Boyce also clearly remembered the interrogation: "When we got off the operation, somebody—a colonel or light colonel—asked us if anything out of the ordinary had taken place. Some sergeant who was there just shook his head. He didn't say yes or no. He didn't say either way. That's the way they [the Army] do it; they usually ask the highest-ranking guy. The officer directed questions at everybody, but the senior man answered. He's supposed to. In training, they try to brainwash you—they tell you that 'you don't ask questions; just obey orders.' " Even Ron Grzesik told Henderson no. As he explained later, "It was the only answer I could think of." Harry Stanley later wondered why the colonel expected anyone to say anything, since "the first thing they teach you is about the chain of command. If I talked to the colonel, they'd [Charlie Company] find some way to get me."

By the afternoon of the eighteenth, Medina was convinced that the matter was indeed closed. Colonel Barker later suggested that he tell the company not to discuss the incident with anyone else—a step Medina had already taken.

John Paul, Medina's radioman, remembered that "we did hear that we were under investigation for what happened, but a few days later I heard—this was just a rumor —that General Westmoreland had given us a job-well-done and it was dropped."

Henderson, meanwhile, concluded his investigation at LZ Dotti. There are again different versions of what took place. Secretary Resor told Congress later that Henderson, during his informal investigation of the incident, "interviewed the Task Force commander and S-3 [Major Calhoun, the executive officer], and the commanders of the two companies which had been in the immediate area. He also received some reports of unnecessary killing through Vietnamese channels." But Henderson, making no mention of Vietnamese reports, told newsmen simply that the answers he received from the men of Charlie Company and Captain Medina "satisfied me and I accepted them." He then made an oral report of his findings to headquarters of the Americal Division. A few days later, around April 1, Henderson personally talked to General Koster about My Lai 4.

By this time Lewellen had played his long-running tape to a number of officers attached to headquarters company at Duc Pho. Lieutenant John Gore, of Lawrenceville, New Jersey, listened to it a few days after the March 16 mission. "It was instant replay," Gore said later. He remembered that

Lewellen continued "to play it once in a while" for the men of the brigade.

Within weeks the local Viet Cong units in Quang Ngai Province began distributing leaflets about the incident. Henderson forwarded some of the material—he called it propaganda—to division headquarters. Koster requested a written report on the incident. The colonel complied in late April by simply putting on paper his earlier findings. He asked no more questions of Charlie Company, later explaining, "This was not an investigation. It was merely a commander looking at the operations and trying to determine whether there was any basis for an investigation . . ." He also decided not to give the men lie-detector tests: "I didn't attempt to tear out more information." In a subsequent written report, Henderson concluded that "approximately twenty noncombatants had been inadvertently killed by preparatory fires and in crossfires between friendly and enemy forces, and that the reports of unnecessary killing of civilians were merely another instance of a command Viet Cong propaganda technique and were groundless." Yet the men of Charlie Company had told the colonel just five weeks earlier that *no* friendly civilians were killed.

Henderson said that sometime in May, 1968, he was ordered by General Koster to conduct a formal inquiry. The practice of formalizing an on-the-spot field investigation is a normal one in the military, but Koster's order to Henderson to handle it was a deviation. Usually a division commander will request his Inspector General's office—charged by regulation with responsibility for such investigations—to step in at that point. Henderson in turn assigned Lieutenant Colonel Barker to handle the formal inquiry, although it was Barker's Task Force that was being investigated. Barker reached the same conclusion as he had, Henderson explained: "Colonel Barker also talked to a number of the men who had been in on this operation, and he also got a negative." Barker's report was deemed satisfactory by Henderson, who signed it and sent it on to headquarters. Whatever Barker did do remains a mystery. Of over forty members of Charlie Company who were later asked about it, none could recall the Barker investigation. Medina himself heard nothing about My Lai 4 after the brief on-the-spot interrogation in March until the Army contacted him in May, 1969, during the Calley investigation.

Once Barker's report was handed in, General Koster should have forwarded it to his superiors in Saigon and Washington. A Defense Department directive then in force said clearly that reports of civilian killings—whether substantiated or not—must be forwarded up the line. Koster's actions throughout the March 16 incident were suspect. The officer, who later became Superintendent of West Point, is known to have been monitoring radio transmissions in the area that day. Most Vietnam combat veterans agree he should have taken it upon himself to at least fly over the My Lai 4 operation—the most significant for the Americal Division at that time. Did he, as Medina claimed, order the captain not to return to the hamlet and do the more accurate count that Major Calhoun was insisting upon? Did he call for an immediate Inspector General's investigation after receiving Henderson's oral report on the My Lai 4 incident? Did he follow the directive about forwarding such reports to his superiors in Saigon? A three-star general was put in charge of a Pentagon investigation in November, 1969, to determine, among other things, the answers to those questions.

A reporter eventually asked Henderson if either he or Barker ever attempted to question any surviving residents of the hamlet. Told no, the reporter persisted: were such interviews simply not possible or just not considered essential to the investigation? "Both," Henderson replied. The colonel also said that neither Medina nor anyone else had instructed the men of Charlie Company not to talk about the massacre.

The South Vietnamese army had much more direct evidence that something had happened in My Lai 4—eyewitness accounts from survivors, a long list of the dead from the hamlet chief, and reports from its own intelligence units saying that approximately 500 villagers were "gathered" together by American GIs and shot down. Nonetheless, not one official in the Vietnamese government was willing publicly—or even privately—to risk the displeasure of the Americans by insisting that the incident be thoroughly investigated.

Within a few days after March 16—the dead had been buried by then—Do Dinh Luyen, the village chief of Song My (which includes the My Lai 4 area), turned over a carefully compiled list of the dead to the official immediately above him in the Vietnamese hierarchy—the Son Tinh district chief, Captain Tran Ngoc Tan. He in turn reported the incident to the Quang Ngai province chief, Colonel Thon That Khien, within a few days. Captain Tan, who made his report by letter, also sent a sharply critical note to the chief of staff of the South Vietnamese 2nd Division, which had responsibility for the area. Included with the note was the list of the 450 to 500 villagers who were said to have been shot. Tan's report put Colonel Khien in an unenviable position; the forty-year-old officer was popular among American military men, who considered him a strong supporter. But Khien knew that no one reporting an American atrocity would remain a friend for long, particularly after a number of high-ranking American officers had already investigated the charges, and ruled them groundless.

Khien delayed. He explained later that he was reluctant to provide the enemy with anything it could use as propaganda, and that he also had doubts the Americans could commit such a crime. He had tried to convince himself that it was an accident—perhaps some artillery had gone astray. In any case, once the Viet Cong began distributing leaflets about the incident, he, of course, had to keep quiet; otherwise he would be providing support for the enemy.

But officials of the South Vietnamese 2nd Division, meanwhile, had started doing what Khien was afraid to do: they were investigating the report. On April 15, four weeks after the incident, military intelligence officials filed reports noting that American troops had "gathered people together" and executed almost 500 of them in the My Lai 4 hamlet of Song My village on March 16. The document was found by a London newspaperman in late 1969 at the province headquarters in Quang Ngai. It was signed by a Colonel Toan, an intelligence staff officer of the 2nd Division, who accompanied his report with a request that province authorities check it out.

At least one American officer heard of the atrocity through this exchange of Vietnamese reports. He, too, dismissed it without asking for an investigation. Captain Angel M. Rodriguez was the assistant district adviser in Son Tinh District at the time. On April 15, the same day the Vietnamese reports were filed, Rodriguez signed a statement dismissing them: "The Song My village chief feels that this action was taken in revenge for an American soldier killed by sniper fire in the village." Other documents further indicated that Rodriguez and other district officials gave Do Dinh Luyen's report little credence. It seemed clear to the officials that the people who provided the information were

Viet Cong or Viet Cong sympathizers; after all, they were living in a Viet Cong-dominated area. The officials had a further reason for doubting the authenticity of the village chief's report—it was based on hearsay. But none of them seemed to consider that the chief, as a government official, would still have reliable sources of information, even though he did not live in the village proper for fear of his life.

A further document, also seen by a reporter at the province headquarters, revealed that in June, Colonel Khien requested Colonel Toan of the 2nd Division and James A. May, the senior United States province adviser at the time, to take up the matter with the Americal Division. That document was the last-known contact at the time between the Americans and the South Vietnamese regarding My Lai 4. May, in an interview, said he left Quang Ngai on May 29, 1968, and had heard nothing of the incident up to then. His successor, Robert T. Burke, insisted that "I never heard a word. Not a thing."

The Song My village chief told a newsman in November, 1969, that he had never spoken to any American about the massacre. And no Americans—either from the province adviser's office or from the Americal Division—ever attempted to verify the chief's report by interrogating survivors. The next discussion about My Lai 4 between Americans and South Vietnamese took place the following spring, when the United States Army launched its investigation.

It's impossible to determine how far up the Vietnamese reports climbed in the bureaucracy. Had normal procedure been followed, Khien's report to the 2nd Division would have been passed up to the corps commander, the Vietnamese joint general staff, the defense minister, the premier, and then to the president. In early December, 1969, President Thieu was reported to have known about the My Lai 4

case for more than a year. It was said that he believed
there was a good deal of truth to it, but did not want to
acknowledge the incident publicly, telling associates at the
time that it would only increase the anti-American feeling
in South Vietnam.

8

The Uncovering—
Part I

*I*т took twenty months for the American public to learn what Charlie Company had done in a few hours at My Lai 4. Why, and how, the deliberate murder of hundreds of civilians remained a secret so long is difficult to understand, especially because so many knew about it—and so many had participated in it.

Dozens of Charlie Company GIs had transferred to other units in South Vietnam—and presumably told many of their new buddies about the day's events at My Lai 4.

GIs talk, and brag; the 250 men in the other two companies of Task Force Barker learned within days about what had happened in My Lai 4. A number of officers in the brigade had listened with fascination to a tape-recording of the events at My Lai 4. At least sixty Army men in a dozen helicopters— gunships assigned by the Americal Division to help Charlie Company overcome the expected Viet Cong resistance—saw first-hand. And there were the survivors, unknown in number, of My Lai 4 itself.

Details of the massacre had been published twice in France: in the May 15, 1968, edition of the French-language publication *Sud Vietnam en Lutte,* and in *Bulletin du Vietnam,* published by the North Vietnamese delegation to the Paris peace talks. The issue was raised again in a report to the July meeting in Grenoble, France, of the World Conference of Jurists for Vietnam.

By the early summer of 1968, Paul Meadlo was home in Terre Haute, Indiana, his right foot gone, along with his self-respect. And by early 1969 most of Charlie Company was gone from Vietnam, back on the job or at school in cities across the nation. Ron Haeberle was busy in Ohio showing slide photographs of the My Lai 4 massacre to Rotary Club luncheons and the like; no one in his audiences apparently cared, or believed, enough to find out how he had managed to take such pictures. But no one else seemed to consider his experiences worth telling about publicly.

But at that time a twenty-two-year-old ex-GI in Phoenix, Arizona, was in the midst of preparing a letter that would eventually prompt an Army investigation of the massacre. Ronald Ridenhour had flown over My Lai 4 a few days after the shootings. He noticed the complete desolation— "not even a bird was singing"—but did not find out what caused it until he joined a long-range reconnaissance unit operating out of Duc Pho, where he heard accounts of the massacre from five eyewitnesses. Ridenhour drove to the Americal Division headquarters in Chu Lai and confirmed that Charlie Company had indeed been at My Lai 4 on March 16. Ridenhour was cautious as he gathered information in Vietnam; he did not even make written notes, for fear of his own safety if they were found.

Ridenhour was discharged and returned to Phoenix in early December, 1968, intent on doing something about the shootings at My Lai 4. He had served well in Vietnam, both as a helicopter door gunner and as a team leader of long-range patrol groups. He earned the usual medals, and did nothing that would mark him as an antiwar protester. He kept his outrage to himself. But "I wanted to get those people," Ridenhour said. "I wanted to reveal what they did. My God, when I first came home, I would tell my friends about this and cry—literally cry. As far as I was concerned, it was a reflection on me, on every American, on the ideals that we supposedly represent. It completely castrated the whole picture of America."

Those to whom he talked urged him not to report it, not to turn in his buddies, not to help the enemy. "Forget about it," one friend said, "if you know what's good for you and America." By the next spring the young ex-GI was hard at work as a popsicle maker for a local ice cream company, saving his money so he could continue his college education in the fall at Claremont Men's College near Los Angeles.

He turned now to Arthur A. Orman, one of his former high school teachers who had also taught him creative writing during the one year he attended Phoenix College before getting drafted. Along with his moral indignation, Ridenhour had another motivation: he'd always wanted to be a writer, and he knew he would never find a better story with which to begin. Orman, however, convinced the ex-GI not to try to sell his story to a magazine. Instead, he argued, Ridenhour should give his information to those government agencies that were equipped to investigate such matters. "I thought it would cheapen what he was doing if he tried to sell the story," Orman said.

Ridenhour agreed; his former instructor was the only person in Phoenix thus far—March, 1969—who had encouraged him to go ahead with his plans to report the men of Charlie Company.

Then came the critical decision to approach Congress. The two men agreed that letters should be sent to leading members of the House and Senate, and not just to the White House, Pentagon and State Department. Orman later explained why: "I had been drafted and worked for the Army's Adjutant General's Corps for a while, and I knew how responsive the Army was to Congress. I'd also been around bureaucracy both in the Army and in the school system long enough to realize that things have a way of getting buried almost immediately, but if they keep coming up, there's a good chance somebody will do something about them."

Orman's secretary was borrowed to type the letter. Thirty copies were reproduced and mailed out. Orman had wanted to send them all by registered mail, but Ridenhour didn't have enough cash for the postage, and refused to take a loan from his former instructor.

The letter described in detail what Ridenhour had learned about My Lai 4, but he was careful to make clear he was reporting what he heard, and not what he saw. The letter said, in part:

It was late in April, 1968, that I first heard of "Pinkville" and what allegedly happened there. I received that first report with some skepticism, but in the following months I was to hear similar stories from such a wide variety of people that it became impossible for me to disbelieve that something rather dark and bloody did occur sometime in March, 1968, in a village called "Pinkville" in the Republic of Vietnam. . . .

In late April, 1968, I was awaiting orders for a transfer . . . when I happened to run into [Charles] "Butch" Gruver, whom I had known in Hawaii [Ridenhour went through training with the 11th Brigade at Schofield Barracks, as did Charlie Company]. . . . During the course of our conversation he told me the first of many reports I was to hear of "Pinkville."

"Charlie" Company . . . had been assigned to Task Force Barker in late February, 1968, to help conduct "search and destroy" operations on the Batangan Peninsula, Barker's area of operations. . . . One village area was particularly troublesome and seemed to be infested with booby traps and enemy soldiers. It was located about six miles northeast of Quang Ngai city. . . . It was a notorious area and the men of Task Force Barker had a special name for it: they called it "Pinkville." One morning in the latter part of March, Task Force Barker moved out from its firebase, headed for "Pinkville." Its mission: destroy the trouble spot and all of its inhabitants.

When "Butch" told me this I didn't quite believe that what he was telling me was true, but he assured me that it was and went on to describe what happened. . . . I asked "Butch" several times if all the people were killed. He said that he thought they were, men, women, and children. . . . Gruver estimated that the population of the village had been 300 to 400 people and that very few, if any, escaped.

After hearing this account I couldn't quite accept it. Somehow I just couldn't believe that not only had so many young American men participated in such an act of barbarism, but that their officers had ordered it. There were other men in the unit I was soon to be assigned to . . . who had been in Charlie Company at the time that Gruver alleged the incident at "Pinkville" had occurred. I became determined to ask them about "Pinkville" so that I might compare their accounts with Gruver's. . . .

The first men I looked for were Michael Terry and William Doherty. Both were veterans of Charlie Company and

"Pinkville." Instead of contradicting Butch Gruver's story, they corroborated it, adding some tasty tidbits of information of their own. . . .

If Terry, Doherty and Gruver could be believed, then not only had "Charlie" Company received orders to slaughter all the inhabitants of the village, but those orders had come from the commanding officer of Task Force Barker, or possibly even higher in the chain of command. . . .

It was June before I spoke to anyone who had something of significance to add to what I had already been told. . . . I ran into Sergeant Larry LaCroix at the USO in Chu Lai. LaCroix had been in 2nd. Lt. Kally's [Calley] platoon on the day Task Force Barker swept through "Pinkville." What he told me verified the stories of the others, but he also had something new to add. He had been a witness to Kally's gunning down of at least three separate groups of villagers. . . .

This account of Sergeant LaCroix's confirmed the rumors that Gruver, Terry and Doherty had previously told me about Lieutenant Kally. It also convinced me that there was a very substantial amount of truth to the stories that all of these had told. If I needed more convincing, I was to receive it.

It was in the middle of November, 1968, just a few weeks before I was to return to the United States for separation from the Army that I talked to Michael Bernhardt. . . . Bernhardt had served his entire year in Vietnam in "Charlie" Company and he too was about to go home. "Bernie" substantiated the tales told by the other men I had talked to in vivid, bloody detail. . . .

Exactly what did, in fact, occur in the village of "Pinkville" in March, 1968, I do not know for *certain,* but I am convinced that it was something very black indeed. I remain irrevocably persuaded that if you and I do truly believe in the principles of justice and the equality of every man, however humble, before the law, that forms the very backbone that this country is founded on, then we must press forward a widespread and public investigation of this matter with all our combined efforts. . . .

I have considered sending this to newspapers, magazines, and broadcasting companies, but I somehow feel that investigation and action by the Congress of the United States is the appropriate procedure, and as a conscientious citizen I have no desire to further besmirch the image of the American servicemen in the eyes of the world. I feel that this action, while probably it would promote attention, would not bring about the constructive actions that the direct actions of the Congress of the United States would.

Nine letters—sent by registered mail—were addressed to President Nixon; three Democratic senators who were then the leading anti-Vietnam war spokesmen in Congress: Eugene J. McCarthy of Minnesota, J. W. Fulbright of Arkansas, and Edward M. Kennedy of Massachusetts; and the five members of the Arizona Congressional delegation: Republican Senators Barry M. Goldwater and Paul J. Fannin, House members Sam Steiger and John J. Rhodes, both Republicans, and Democrat Morris K. Udall. Letters were also sent by ordinary air mail to the Pentagon, State Department, Joint Chiefs of Staff, thirteen other members of the Senate, three members of the House, including Chairman L. Mendel Rivers of the Armed Services Committee, and to the House and Senate chaplains.

Thousands of letters pour into official Washington every day, many of them the work of cranks. Even serious letters, if they are mimeographed or Xeroxed, rarely receive the attention of a busy legislator; they are either routinely answered by his office, or ignored.

Twenty-two of the offices later said they had no record of ever receiving Ridenhour's letter. The Reverend Edward Gardiner Latch, Chaplain of the House, read the Xeroxed letter, but said later he did not answer it because "I don't

answer letters of that kind." Five legislators—Congressmen
Rhodes and Steiger of Arizona, and Senators Edward W.
Brooke of Massachusetts and Goldwater and Fannin of
Arizona—routinely referred it to the Army.

Only two men, Representatives Morris Udall, a liberal
from Arizona, and L. Mendel Rivers, a conservative from
South Carolina, took a personal interest in the letter. In
both cases, their concern was the result of alert staff work.

When Ridenhour's letter arrived at the office of the
Armed Services Committee, it was read by Frank Slatinshek,
a staff lawyer, who took it to his superior, Chief Counsel
John R. Blandford. "We couldn't brush it off," Blandford
recalled later. "It had too many facts. There was too much
of a germ of truth in it." A letter was drafted for Rivers'
signature, urging the Department of the Army to investigate
the matter, and Rivers signed it on April 7, only three days
after it was received by the Committee.

One factor behind Rivers' quick action may have been
Udall. Ridenhour had included Udall on his list of thirty
largely because he represented his home state, and to a
lesser degree because of Udall's political views. Both factors were important to what happened next. Udall was especially impressed by Ridenhour's letter, which was brought
to his attention by Roger Lewis, an aide. "It just had a ring
to it," Lewis said. "Furthermore, he was an Arizonan."

The aide suggested it might not be the work of a crackpot. "It's funny," Udall recalled. "I think if both of us had
said, 'Oh, what the hell, just another crackpot letter,' there
might have been a whitewash of this at Defense." Udall
wrote a letter to Secretary of Defense Melvin A. Laird about
Ridenhour's charges, and took the unusual step of sending
a copy to Rivers. Udall knew that any military investigation
would have a better chance of being held if Rivers pushed
it, and he thought Rivers might just—out of legislative

courtesy—push. "He likes me," Udall said of Rivers. "I know my letter personally came to his attention. I think the standing I had with him was probably a factor. It was just one of these decisions that could have gone several other ways." Udall was convinced that if only he alone wrote, the Pentagon would refer Ridenhour's letter to a public affairs officer in Vietnam, and nothing more would come of it. "But when Rivers, the committee chairman, wrote, it made a difference," the congressman explained. Rivers' outspoken support of the military on almost all defense issues made him a prime target of peace groups, but he maintained— with a not unsurprising Southern courtesy—excellent personal relations with many liberal House colleagues. Udall's letter reached the Armed Services Committee on April 7, the same day on which Rivers forwarded his letter to the Department of the Army.

There was additional pressure on the Army—from Secretary of Defense Laird, who later told newsmen he read Ridenhour's letter on April 4, three days before Rivers' request for an investigation was mailed out. Laird recognized that it was "more than a routine letter," an aide said, and immediately forwarded it to the Department of the Army for handling. Laird's personal reading of the letter—one of thousands that arrive every day at the Pentagon—wasn't unusual, the aides explained; he often dealt directly with citizen complaints. However, Laird's subsequent account surprised John Blandford of the Armed Services Committee, who said he distinctly had received the impression from the Army "that the first they knew of this was when we sent over Ridenhour's letter."

The personal pressure from Rivers and Udall may not even have been necessary. By April 10 the Army had received six Congressional referrals enclosing the Ridenhour letter; clearly the military had to do something to avoid a public black eye. Udall was visited by a Pentagon officer soon after he mailed his letter; the officer "immediately promised an investigation." Precisely what the Army thought about Ridenhour's complaints at that time is unknown, but one general familiar with such investigations later commented that "any of us at the start would have thought it was a lot of baloney. There's less of that kind of stuff in Vietnam than in any other war we've had."

On April 12, less than two weeks after he sent his letters, Ridenhour received a reply from Colonel John G. Hill, Jr., of the Army Chief of Staff's office, saying: "Because the circumstances related in your letter concern events of a year or so ago, a proper investigation will take some time. This investigation is under way now." The letter also thanked Ridenhour "for bringing this matter to our attention."

A few days later the Army said in a letter to Congressman Udall that an attempt to investigate the matter from Saigon would be impractical, "as the people involved have since departed Vietnam and are now widely scattered. . . . Faced with these circumstances and considering the gravity of the allegation, it has been determined that a complete investigation will be required." On April 23 General Westmoreland, then Army Chief of Staff, officially turned over the case to the office of the Inspector General, the Army's main investigatory agency for administrative and procedural complaints, and directed it to make a full-scale inquiry. Colonel William Vickers Wilson, a Southerner, was assigned the task of building the Army's case.

Wilson began at the beginning; he flew into Phoenix on April 29 with a court reporter to question Ridenhour. He told Ridenhour, as he would tell others he interrogated, that he was conducting a special investigation for General Westmoreland, Wilson and Ridenhour carefully went over the allegations during an interview in a downtown hotel that lasted one and a half hours. The former GI was told that if Wilson could find corroboration of the charges from just one other witness, a more intensive investigation would be ordered—with the ultimate aim of filing criminal charges against those responsible. Ridenhour was worried after the session—Wilson had seemed a little bit skeptical: "He shook my hand, patted me on the back and sent me on my way, assuring me that I would have a full report from the Department of the Army in four to five weeks."

Wilson, operating in official secrecy, then began a cross-country journey. He interviewed Michael Terry in Orem, Utah, immediately after seeing Ridenhour; Terry told how he had shot and killed some wounded Vietnamese civilians in the drainage ditch at My Lai 4. Wilson tried to find Charles Gruver of Oklahoma City, but could not. He saw Michael Bernhardt on May 8 in Washington, and received further confirmation of the details in Ridenhour's letter. He called on others in the Inspector General's office for help, and statements from other Charlie Company members began flooding in. On May 13 Wilson himself flew to Fort Benning, Georgia, and interrogated Captain Medina. Medina was stunned; he was then in the midst of a nine-month career officers' advanced course that would enable him to get his promotion to major. Since leaving Charlie Company, Medina had been marked for advancement, handling key staff assignments with the 1st Battalion in Vietnam and later with the Americal Division's tactical operations center. He had left Charlie Company, he said later, thinking, "We had a good combat record."

While Wilson worked, Ridenhour worried. He wondered if any of the witnesses named in his letter would confirm the essential details of the massacre. He had reason to believe that most of the persons quoted in his letter were implicated in some manner in the killings. His star witness, he thought, would be Michael Bernhardt. When they had talked in Chu Lai, where Bernhardt was recovering from a severe case of jungle rot on his feet, Ridenhour had sought assurance that Bernhardt would verify his story at the proper time. The GI said he would. Ridenhour began placing collect calls to Colonel Wilson, asking what was going on. He called sometimes twice a week during April and May, but got no information. The lack of news was suspicious, Ridenhour thought; perhaps the Pentagon would whitewash the whole business.

Ridenhour's desire for information collided with the Army's need for secrecy as it investigated the case. By coincidence, Ridenhour called Colonel Wilson in Washington during his May 8 interview with Bernhardt. The colonel was abrupt. Bernhardt was there then, he said, but he had not yet received any significant corroboration of Ridenhour's allegations. He told Ridenhour not to be impatient, and indicated that it would take at least two more months to accumulate the necessary data to complete a report. Wilson also told Ridenhour that he had gathered the names of 60 to 70 percent of the men of Charlie Company and planned to get statements from them as soon as possible. He also would have to go to Vietnam. He assured Ridenhour again that the Army would pursue the case to its limit, and repeated a request that no public mention of the investigation be made.

On May 10 Ridenhour called Bernhardt and learned that he had indeed corroborated the fact of a massacre, telling Colonel Wilson all he knew about it. At this point Ridenhour remembered that the colonel had stated (during his interview with Ridenhour in late April) that if only one corroborating witness could be found, a more intensive investigation would be ordered. In Ridenhour's eyes, Wilson had not kept his word, and he believed that the colonel was only stalling for time while the Army sought a means of covering up the incident. His trust shaken, Ridenhour decided the only thing to do then was to try to make public the details of what had happened at My Lai 4.

On May 29 Ridenhour picked up a writer's guide to literary agents and found one whose blurb seemed sympathetic. Michael Cunningham, a twenty-two-year-old part-time literary agent in Hartford, Connecticut, had indicated his interest in "anything of an unusual or experimental nature," a phrase he acknowledged was written with little thought a few years earlier. Ridenhour mailed Cunningham a copy of his letter, with this comment: "It is my belief that the U.S. Army will, if at all possible, cover up this incident, hoping that it will fade away and be forgotten. I believe very strongly that this should not be allowed to happen."

Ridenhour was basing his belief about a cover-up on flimsy evidence, fed in part by the Army's inability—or unwillingness—to brief him fully on the progress of its investigation. Since Cunningham did not personally know many editors or publishers, he sent telegrams over the next six weeks to a number of magazines, including *Life, Look, Ramparts, Harper's,* and the Washington Post Company (owners of *Newsweek*). The wires quoted part of Ridenhour's letter and asked if the editors were interested in details of the massacre. Only *Ramparts* responded, but Ridenhour did not want to be associated with the violently anti-Vietnam war politics of the magazine.

Ridenhour's persistent inquiries resulted in another report from the Pentagon, this one informing him that about 70 percent of the persons cited in his letter had been interviewed. Ridenhour was not reassured by that information: only eight persons had been named in his letter. The Pentagon also noted that "the investigation is requiring consid-

erable time and travel." To Ridenhour, it seemed like another stall. H got in touch with Udall's office and complained that the Army was burying the case. Udall's aide,
Roger Lewis, began to think—it was now early June—that
he might have been mistaken in assuming that Ridenhour
was not a crackpot. "We still had nothing from the military," Lewis explained later, "no way of knowing. And the
fact that it hadn't broken led one to wonder whether Ridenhour's information was good." Surely a massacre of that
magnitude, and a Pentagon investigation of it, would have
been leaked to the Washington press corps by then. Lewis
decided to telephone Captain Medina. Medina was polite
but firm: he couldn't discuss the case. Lewis then called
Bernhardt and was told that he had indeed been interrogated by the office of the IG. The aide decided that the
Army was trying its best to investigate the Ridenhour
charges, whether they were accurate or not.

By then Colonel Wilson had been working full time on
the case for nearly five weeks.

9

The Uncovering —
Part II

A T 8:30 A.M. on June 13, 1969, the Inspector
General's office of the Army staged a police line-up
at the new Forrestal Defense Building in southwest
Washington. One of the officers in the line-up was
Lieutenant William L. Calley, Jr.

Calley had been abruptly pulled out of Vietnam
in early June—at least one month before his tour
of duty was over—and shipped home overnight to
Fort Benning, Georgia, with special orders to report
to Washington. Calley had been forewarned of
trouble when the Army turned down his request to
extend his tour of duty in Vietnam for a third time.
He knew then, he recalled later, that something was
up.

The line-up was called by Colonel Wilson to
enable a key witness to the massacre—Warrant Officer Hugh C. Thompson of the 123rd Aviation
Battalion—to identify the young officer who had
been directing operations at the bloody drainage

ditch at My Lai 4. Wilson had brought Thompson to the Pentagon on June 11, and quizzed him repeatedly about the lieutenant who had said to Thompson at My Lai that the only way to remove civilians from a bunker was with a hand grenade. On June 12, according to a transcript of Wilson's interrogation, the warrant officer was told he would have a chance to identify the officer: "What we are trying to do is establish if one of these individuals . . . was one of the people that you talked to. This could mean two things. It could either place them at the location of this ditch, depending on which one it is, or establish that that person was not at the ditch at the time you sat down [in the helicopter]." Thompson was assured that his identification "may do as much to clear an individual . . . as it would to accuse someone of being there, so you shouldn't take the attitude [that] this is going to mean too much."

The next morning Thompson picked out Calley as the officer at the drainage ditch in My Lai 4 on March 16, 1968. That fact was duly recorded by an Army stenographer.

Thompson also had reported seeing a captain shoot a woman at close range during that same day. Wilson now turned to that charge. He had received Medina's explanation of the event during his interview with the captain on May 13 at Fort Benning.

"Could you identify the man who shot the girl?" Wilson asked Thompson.

"I think it was a captain, sir . . ."

Without mentioning Medina by name, Wilson then read the pilot Medina's version of the shooting. "Now could this have happened?" he asked.

". . . nothing is impossible," Thompson said. He added that he saw Medina back at LZ Dotti two days after the action in My Lai 4. "He asked me how everything was going and I said, 'Everything is going just fine,' and saluted him and walked away." He said nothing else to Medina, Thompson said, "because I didn't care anything about talking to him." *

On June 19 Wilson interrogated Larry Colburn, who corroborated Thompson's testimony and also identified Medina and Calley as the officers involved in the shootings. Colburn picked out the Charlie Company officers from photographs shown by Wilson; the ex-GI also was shown detailed aerial maps of My Lai 4. Wilson then began interrogating Medina's radiomen and others in his command post who had knowledge of the captain's movements that day. On June 23, for example, John T. Paul, who handled the company radio on March 16, 1968, was told to report to the Pentagon. Paul said that he wasn't sure which of two events he would be asked about: the My Lai 4 massacre, or the time—months afterward—that a junior officer in Charlie Company pulled a gun on three men who refused to descend a hill during a night maneuver.

Throughout this period Ridenhour was still bombarding Wilson with phone calls. But the colonel, by then concluding his investigation, would tell him nothing. Near the end

* On October 15, 1969, four months after his testimony at the Pentagon, Thompson was awarded the Distinguished Flying Cross for heroism in the line of duty at My Lai 4. The citation credited Thompson with "disregarding his own safety" to rescue fifteen children hiding in a bunker "between Viet Cong positions and advancing friendly forces." He also was credited with locating and saving a wounded Vietnamese child "caught in the intense crossfire." The only threats to Thompson that day, of course, were posed by his fellow American GIs. Copies of the citation later made available to reporters at the Pentagon were dated July 1, 1968, slightly more than three months after the action—a normal time lag. But Thompson did not receive the honor for another sixteen months, which suggests that perhaps Colonel Wilson or other officials of the Inspector General's office at the Pentagon, after hearing Thompson's testimony, had recommended him for the award, which was then predated.

of July, Wilson began writing his final report and ordered his office to stop taking these collect calls. "They weren't saying anything . . . just yes, hello, how are you, we can't say a damn thing, goodbye," Ridenhour complained.

Colonel Wilson and other officers in the Inspector General's office had interrogated thirty-six witnesses by the end of July, ranging from Colonel Henderson, the 11th Brigade commander, to Paul Meadlo, whose extraordinary confession was considered to be most significant. The evidence was mounting swiftly against Calley, and on July 23 Wilson was authorized to order Colonel James D. Kiersey, chief of staff at Fort Benning, to "flag" Calley's records, an Army procedure freezing any promotion or transfer for a soldier. Wilson's lengthy report was submitted to General Westmoreland, and on August 4 Westmoreland responded by ordering the Inspector General's office to turn over the results of its investigation to the Provost Marshal's office of the Army and its Criminal Investigation Division to determine whether there was enough evidence to file criminal charges against Calley and others in the company.

Once the C.I.D. took over the case, its men retraced Colonel Wilson's steps and again began to interrogate all of the available members of Charlie Company to determine how many GIs or ex-GIs were implicated. Many of the investigators became personally involved in the investigation. Michael Bernhardt said that he was visited three times by C.I.D. agents who were trying to pry out the truth about Medina's shooting of the woman. "They asked me two times about it, and I didn't say anything. On the third time they said somebody knew that I was there when it happened; somebody had seen me. They started digging and digging into this one. I didn't really feel like saying anything against Medina. I didn't really want to bring anybody's name into it." He felt hostile toward the Army agents: "They've [C.I.D.

agents] never been in combat. They don't know what it's like."

On August 25 the C.I.D. agents found Ronald Haeberle in Cleveland, and he gave them a set of his color photographs of the shootings. Haeberle had been discharged shortly after the My Lai 4 incident; upon his return to the States he had assembled his best photographs into a slide show, which he screened, upon request, for civic organizations in Cleveland. Haeberle's series of photographs began with the 11th Brigade in training at Schofield Barracks in Hawaii, and moved with the unit to Vietnam. Then, amidst pictures of smiling peasants and GIs, came the scenes from My Lai 4. "They caused no commotion," he said. "Nobody believed it. They said Americans wouldn't do this." Haeberle also told the military police agents that as far as he knew, his unprinted rolls of black-and-white film were still lying around the public information office of brigade headquarters. The C.I.D. immediately sent someone to check; the film was there.

By the end of August interrogations of former Charlie Company members were being conducted all over the United States and in Vietnam.* Many witnesses were quizzed a second time and shown the Haeberle photographs. The photos jogged memories, and the GIs began recalling in more detail what happened.

On August 8, four months after the Army first received the Ridenhour letter, Major General William A. Becker, chief of the Congressional liaison for the Army, began giving oral briefings on the My Lai 4 case to members of Con-

---

* The C.I.D. interviewed more than seventy-five witnesses by November 26, 1969. Many of them recalled being asked about the use of marijuana in Charlie Company; that question seemed to be of special interest to the investigators. The GIs all acknowledged that many members of the company smoked or otherwise made use of marijuana, which is plentiful in South Vietnam, but none believed it was in any way a significant factor in what happened at My Lai 4.

gress. L. Mendel Rivers was visited first. On August 11 Becker and Colonel Wilson interviewed Congressman Udall, who said, "They came to say that there was something to the Ridenhour story. They said charges would be brought, and that it would take some time to draft them and make arrests. They hoped I wouldn't do anything publicly about it." Congressman Udall was being handled very carefully, with full colonels visiting him at his office from time to time to assure him that the Army was proceeding properly with the case. "I was in a position to have grandstanded on this for several months if I wanted to," Udall said later. "They [colonels] would keep on reporting, saying they were making an investigation, no stone was being unturned. They'd ask, 'Are you happy?' "

While the Army was preparing its case against him, Lieutenant Calley found himself a lawyer, George W. Latimer of Salt Lake City. The elderly Latimer was highly regarded in military legal circles, having served for ten years on the Military Court of Appeals in Washington and also on the Utah State Supreme Court. Latimer was defending one of the eight Green Berets in connection with another controversial murder charge in mid-1969 when Calley first approached him. He was immediately impressed by the young lieutenant and agreed, as a matter of principle, to take the case. "Why, he could have been my son," Latimer declared in a later interview. "You couldn't ask for a nicer boy." Calley said he used his life savings to hire the Utah lawyer, paying him a retainer of more than $6,000. By November the officer was complaining that he was broke.

As he studied the case, Latimer subsequently explained, he became convinced that Calley was guilty of nothing more than following orders "a little bit too diligently. I don't care whether Calley used the best judgment or not," the lawyer added. "He was faced with a tough decision." Medina's hold on Calley was so strong, the lawyer said, that "if he had ordered Bill [Calley] to lead the platoon up a mountain and jump off it, he would do it."

It was now evident that the Army would have to institute proceedings against Calley. As one military source later explained: "If they don't prosecute somebody for this, the Army's going to get clobbered. And if the story ever breaks without the Army taking any action, it would be even worse." On August 19 Colonel Wilson flew down to Fort Benning to brief the legal officers there about the case. Under Army regulations, the commanding officer of Fort Benning and his legal staff were the ultimate authority for reviewing the evidence and filing charges against Calley, but the Pentagon wanted to make sure that the infantrymen at Benning knew exactly what was going on. A few days earlier the Pentagon had notified the officials at Benning by telegram that Calley must be charged with a general court-martial—a military proceeding for more serious offenses, such as murder—in order to retain him in the service beyond September 6, the day his two years' obligation ended. Wilson brought along a number of statements, including Meadlo's, and the officers reviewed them together. Captain William R. Hill was then the legal officer for the Student Brigade at Fort Benning, the unit to which Calley was attached. Hill was upset by what he learned about Calley that day; statements such as "a ditch filled with bodies" convinced him that Calley was guilty of mass murder.

By then it was clear in Washington that the Army was going to have an unprecedented murder case on its hands, one that could become an international liability and might even affect the progress of the war in South Vietnam.

In late August, Defense Secretary Laird, who had been kept abreast of the case by the Department of the Army, flew to the Summer White House at San Clemente, California, and handed over a detailed summary of Colonel Wilson's findings to the President. Nixon was reportedly angered by the Army's delay in finding out about and investigating the massacre.

The Army cautiously waited for the President to study the documents and react—if he chose to. In late August, Colonel Kiersey—the Fort Benning chief of staff—was ordered to "hold" the processing of charges against Calley because "you may be receiving additional instructions through channels." The order came from four-star General James K. Woolnough, the commanding general of the Continental Army Command at Fort Monroe, Virginia. The delay nearly precipitated a staff revolt among the young legal officers at Benning, some of whom were fearful that the Administration would decide not to charge Calley with the murders. But the young officers also knew that under the Military Code of Justice, the Army had the right to disregard the White House and other superiors and ask for a court-martial anyway. Many of the officers would have wanted to sign the murder charges against Calley, and Captain Hill, a non-career officer, talked briefly about flipping a coin with them to determine who would, but then decided, as a matter of principle, to sign the charge sheet himself. Hill also urged his immediate superior, Colonel Lon D. Marlowe, to go ahead with the trial even if he had to defy the Pentagon. Hill was convinced that the Army was reluctant to charge Calley because of the potential propaganda advantage to the Viet Cong. But Marlowe, about to retire from the service, was cautious. "You know the President is involved in this?" he asked Hill. The captain did know by then, as did most of the legal officers at Fort Benning, that Laird had taken a report on the case to the President at the Summer White House, and that there had been a "hold" placed on further proceedings.

There was no opportunity to challenge the White House, however, because on September 4, two days before Calley was to be released from the Army, Fort Benning officials were told to go ahead and file the charges, if they were so determined. "It's all yours," a general told Colonel Kiersey. "You are not receiving any instructions."

On the next day charges were formally preferred against Calley. Six specifications of premeditated murder were drawn up, accusing Calley of killing a total of 109 "Oriental human beings, occupants of the village of My Lai 4, whose names and sexes are unknown, by means of shooting them with a rifle." Preparing the charge sheet had been a difficult task: at one time the Army planned to charge Calley with only four specifications. The officer who wrote the charges, Colonel Robert M. Lathop, chief legal official at Fort Benning, had flown to Washington in August to get assistance in drafting the language. Lathop said that many of the specific charges were based on Paul Meadlo's statements.*

Once the charges were filed, the Army immediately began an Article 32 hearing to determine whether the charges were justified. This kind of hearing is a phenomenon of military law, roughly equivalent to a grand jury proceeding, in which the evidence against a suspect is weighed to determine whether or not he should stand trial. At that time Calley refused to testify against Captain Medina, his commanding officer, and continued to refuse in subsequent legal proceedings. Asked later to explain this refusal, he said

---

* The charges were later reduced to 102 on February 6, 1970, after Calley's lawyers protested that they were too broadly drawn. The Army also made clear in subsequent pretrial hearings that it was not accusing Calley personally of killing each of the Vietnamese victims, but with killing some and "causing others" to kill them.

cryptically, "Because I don't scare easily." Sergeant Isaiah
Cowen, one of Calley's sergeants in the first platoon, was
a witness at the Article 32 hearing and also refused to
testify against Medina "because he was the company commander."

Calley's refusal to testify against Medina was apparently
based on his strong sense of loyalty, both to Medina and
the military, but the Army thought there might be a different
reason. Calley later said that Major Kenneth A. Raby of
Fort Benning, his appointed military legal officer, unsuccessfully tried on at least one or two occasions to persuade
him to take a sanity test.

Ridenhour—the man responsible for instigating the investigation—still did not know what was going on at this
point. On August 6 the Department of the Army had sent
him a letter which discussed only one of his original charges:
that Medina had prevented Michael Bernhardt from writing
his congressman about My Lai. The letter said that the
allegation had been "substantiated in part," adding that
Bernhardt had testified that "Captain Medina did not order
but encouraged him not to write his congressman." The
communication did little to pacify Ridenhour—if that was
its intent. Ridenhour wrote Congressman Udall on August
13: "I can only look upon this letter as either a failure by
the Department of the Army to uncover the truth or as a
blatant attempt by them to 'play down' or conceal the
truth. . . ." By then Udall and his aide, Roger Lewis,
knew—on an official basis—that charges would be filed.
Lewis wrote Ridenhour, trying to reassure him: "There is
reason to believe a significant development is in the works."

But Ridenhour was disheartened; it had been more than
three months since Colonel Wilson first interviewed him,
and nothing seemed to be happening. He went again to
Arthur Orman in Phoenix, seeking more advice. "I thought

we could maybe blanket the entire Congress with another letter," Orman said later. "You know, all he'd need was a ream of paper and twenty dollars' worth of stamps." But Ridenhour delayed; some instinct must have made him hesitate. In early September, Colonel Wilson finally called him and told him that Lieutenant Calley had been arrested and that he would be charged in connection with the murder of an unspecified number of civilians in Vietnam.

The House Armed Services Committee was also told at the same time by the Department of the Army of its action against Calley. "We are exercising utmost caution," a communiqué said, "to avoid any public discussion which could prejudice the continuing investigation or the rights of Lieutenant Calley."

The Pentagon, well aware of the potential impact of the story, debated how to release it to the public. It found a way that managed to bring no credit either to the military—or to the press.

10

The Press

*T*HE first public hint of the My Lai 4 massacre was a blandly worded news release issued to the Georgia press on Friday afternoon, September 5, by the public information office at Fort Benning. It said, in full:

> 1LT William L. Calley, Jr., is being retained on active duty beyond his normal release date because of an investigation being conducted under Article 32 of the Uniform Code of Military Justice.
>
> 1LT Calley, who was to have been separated from the Army on 6 Sep. 69, is charged with violation of Article 118, murder, for offenses allegedly committed against civilians while serving in Vietnam in March 1968.
>
> Whether the matter will be referred to trial by court-martial will be determined by the Commanding General, Fort Benning, upon completion of the Article 32 investigation. In order not to prejudice the continuing investigation and the rights of the accused, it is not appropriate to report further details at this time.

The press release did not state that six specifications of murder had been laid against the young lieutenant, nor did it state that he was accused of murdering, by deliberately shooting with a rifle, 109 Vietnamese civilians. There is nothing in military law that precluded the release of such information. The Army said that publication of the specific charges would jeopardize Calley's rights.

As released, the fact that Calley was being kept in the service because of pending murder charges was a routine story. A reporter in Georgia for the Associated Press asked for more information and was referred to the Pentagon, where he was told that no further details were available. The AP's subsequent dispatch did no more than repeat the essential facts as released by Fort Benning. The wire service story was published in dozens of newspapers over the weekend, but none gave it prominence. *The New York Times*, for example, published an edited version of the AP story at the bottom of page 38 of its September 8 editions.

Calley's plight received more attention in Columbus, Georgia, where the local newspapers published it on page 1. Charles Black, military writer for the morning *Columbus Enquirer,* went to visit Calley—the only reporter in the nation to do so at that time—but the young lieutenant refused to discuss the case.

In Miami, Calley's hometown, an editor of the *Miami Herald* assigned an experienced reporter, Arnold Markowitz, to follow up the story. Markowitz quickly dug out some old clips about Calley's problems as a railroad switchman, and telephoned Colonel Douglas Tucker, an information officer at Fort Benning, to see if the Calley who had disrupted rush-hour traffic in Fort Lauderdale, Florida, was the same Calley who was now accused of murder. Tucker checked, and called back to say they were indeed the same. "Listen, is it one, or two, or three—how many did he kill?" Markowitz abruptly asked the officer. "No comment" was the answer. The reporter later said that "I wasn't thinking of any guys doing anything like this [My Lai 4]. I just wanted to know if he shot up a gin mill in Saigon, or what." Markowitz's story was published on page 9 the next morning.

Officers in the Pentagon were prepared for a flood of questions that weekend from all news media—but it didn't come. "I was amazed that it didn't get picked up— just amazed," said one colonel. Secretary of Defense Melvin A. Laird later revealed that he had ordered the news wires monitored to see if the announcement would spark immediate controversy. He was informed that the Associated Press ran its story on Calley sixty-two minutes before its main competitor, United Press International.

Five days after the original announcement, the news of Calley's arrest was telecast on the Huntley-Brinkley nightly evening news show. Robert Goralski, NBC's Pentagon correspondent, told the millions of viewers that Calley "has been accused of premeditated murder of a number of South Vietnamese civilians. The murders are alleged to have been committed a year ago and the investigation is continuing. A growing number of such cases is coming to light and the Army doesn't know what to do about them."

For weeks there was nothing more in the press about Calley, but the Army continued to gather evidence for his court-martial. Paul Meadlo, the most important prosecution witness, was interviewed for a third time by C.I.D. agents on September 18 at his home in Terre Haute. And Captain Lewellen decided at about that time to turn over his tapes of the radio traffic above My Lai 4 to the prosecution at Fort Benning. He kept a few copies for himself, however.*

---

* Later Lewellen explained that he was planning to sell the tape to the highest bidder as soon as the court proceedings against Charlie Company were completed. "It paints a picture," Lewellen said of his recording.

Ridenhour, meanwhile, became convinced that the Army's failure to publicize details of the case against Calley meant not only that "Calley was going to get hung as a scapegoat" but higher-ranking officers who passed down the order to Calley would get off without a reprimand. He also suspected that the Army would make a deal with Calley, through his lawyers, "to keep him quiet." On October 13 the Army again wrote Ridenhour, telling him that Calley's Article 32 hearing on the murder charges would begin that month, and noting: "It is not appropriate to report details of the allegations to news media. Your continued cooperation in this matter is acknowledged."

Ridenhour, of course, continued to urge his agent to help tell the whole story, but on October 22 Michael Cunningham wrote Ridenhour, conceding defeat: "Quite frankly, Ron, I am doubtful of my ability to be of much more help. I honestly feel that matter is best handled at this stage by waiting until your next response from the Army." At this point Ridenhour decided to give his file to a newspaper reporter. He got the name of Ben Cole, a Washington reporter for the Phoenix, Arizona, *Republic* through Congressman Udall's office. "They said he had gotten wind of the thing and was interested," Ridenhour said. "I called the guy in D.C. and explained it to him and said, 'Are you interested? Will you put it in the paper?' and he said, 'Yeah, yeah, yeah.'"

By then, in late October, there was another reporter who also had dug up many of the important details of the Calley case. Charles Black of the *Columbus Enquirer* had noticed that Calley was wearing the patch of the Americal Division when Black had interviewed him in September; Black continued to piece together information from former Vietnam veterans of that division who were stationed at Fort Benning. But Black, who had gone to Vietnam five

times for his newspaper, decided not to print anything until
the Army spoke out about the case. He didn't want to
embarrass the Army. "Next to Jim Lucas [of the Scripps-
Howard newspaper syndicate], I guess I'm the Army's
favorite newspaperman," he said later.

Cole missed the story because, as he recalled, he just
didn't have time to begin research on it. "Ridenhour gave
it to me just before I came down with a bad cold in October. . . . I was a sick baby." When Ridenhour telephoned
a few weeks later to find out why the story hadn't broken,
Cole was irritated. "He just sat on the goddamn thing,"
Ridenhour said.

Details of the charges against Calley were now known
to dozens of officials—Senator John C. Stennis and his
shocked Senate Armed Services Committee were given a
private briefing that fall—yet nothing reached the press.
Despite the widespread official knowledge of the Calley
case, a few Pentagon officers actually thought Calley could
be court-martialed without attracting any significant public
attention. The opinion was far from unanimous, however.
Perhaps anticipating a future furor over My Lai 4, General Westmoreland included these unusual words during a
speech on October 14 to the annual meeting of the Association of the U. S. Army in Washington: "Recently, a few
individuals involved in serious incidents have been high-
lighted in the news. Some would have these incidents reflect
on the Army as a whole. They are, however, the actions of
a pitiful few. Certainly the Army cannot and will not
condone improper conduct or criminal acts—I personally
assure you that I will not."

The Calley case remained dormant as far as the press
was concerned until the inevitable Washington tipsters got
to work. *The New York Times* heard something about a
massacre case being tried at Fort Gordon, Georgia. It was

the right case, but the wrong base. The *Washington Post* queried the Pentagon about some officer's being charged with more than 150 civilian murders in connection with a Vietnam operation. One *Post* reporter even managed to locate George W. Latimer, Calley's attorney, at his Salt Lake City office, and ask him about the case. Latimer begged off, saying, "I'm hoping maybe we can come up with some kind of resolution that won't make it necessary for this to be public. I can't see it would do any good to anybody." No news story was written.

I, the author of this book, was in the midst of completing research for a book on the Pentagon when I received a telephone tip on October 22. "The Army's trying to court-martial some guy in secret at Fort Benning for killing seventy-five Vietnamese civilians," the source said. At that time, in fact, the Army had done nothing more than prefer charges, and it was still trying to keep any word about the events at My Lai 4 out of the newspapers. It took two days and twenty-five telephone calls before somebody told me about the AP story on Calley. From there, it was a short step to Latimer, and on October 29, a Monday, I flew from Washington to Salt Lake City to interview the lawyer. Before leaving Washington, I had received confirmation of the essential facts of the story from a government source. Latimer confirmed them, adding that: "Whatever killing there was was in a firefight in connection with an operation. To me," Latimer said, "the thing that's important is this: why do we prosecute our own people while on a search-and-destroy mission and they kill some people, be they civilian or not? Is there a point in the chain of command at which somebody could be tried? I think not."

On November 11, a Tuesday, I decided to fly down to Fort Benning and find Calley. But Calley's name did not appear anywhere in the Fort Benning telephone book, nor did the file of tenants in the bachelor officers' quarters list him. It was ten hours afterward and very late at night before I found a warrant officer, who was a downstairs neighbor of Calley's, at one of the officers' quarters. As we were talking, he suddenly hollered at a slight young man walking toward us—"Rusty, come over here and meet this guy." Impatient, I began to leave. "No, wait a second," the officer said. "That's Calley."

Calley was apprehensive. All he wanted in life was to stay in the Army and be a good soldier. He reminded me of an earnest freshman one might find at an agricultural college, anxious about making a fraternity. We went to a party at a friend's apartment and had some drinks. I wanted to leave. Calley wanted me to stay. He knew what was coming and he knew I was the last reporter to whom he would talk, and drink with, for many months. He told me, that evening, a little bit about the operation; he also told me how many people he had been accused of killing. I flew back to Washington the next day and began to write my story. I did it somewhat hesitantly, my thought being that Calley, perhaps, was as much of a victim as those infants he and his men murdered at My Lai 4.

The first story began: "Lieutenant William L. Calley, Jr., twenty-six, is a mild-mannered, boyish-looking Vietnam combat veteran with the nickname of 'Rusty.' The Army says he deliberately murdered at least 109 Vietnamese civilians during a search-and-destroy mission in March, 1968, in a Viet Cong stronghold known as 'Pinkville.' "

Once I had completed my research on My Lai 4, I tried to get it published. *Life* and *Look* magazines weren't interested. With some hesitation, I turned over my story to the Dispatch News Service, a small Washington news agency managed by David Obst. He was twenty-three years old, but his enthusiasm more than made up for his lack of experience. Fifty newspapers were offered the initial Dispatch story by cable on November 12; more than thirty— including many of the leading newspapers in the nation— published it the next day, a remarkably high number.

Even more remarkable, however, was the fact that only *The New York Times* chose to pursue the story at its most logical point—South Vietnam. Most newspapers contented themselves with printing a later AP dispatch saying only that "Army officials say they have completed an investigation into charges of multiple murder of Vietnamese civilians by a young American lieutenant, but that a decision whether to try him remains to be made." The Pentagon refused to comment on the Dispatch story.

In Saigon, Henry Kamm, the *Times'* roving correspondent in Southeast Asia, was assigned to locate the victimized village, which was identified only as "Pinkville" in the first Dispatch account. Kamm bribed his way on a commercial flight to Da Nang, and ended up in Quang Ngai City a few hours later. But he couldn't find out which hamlet was "Pinkville." On the next day he drove to the Americal Division headquarters at Chu Lai, and ran into André C. R. Feher, an investigator for the C.I.D., who "lectured me in a heavy German accent as to why he couldn't tell me anything." By Saturday, November 15, the Army gave in to the inevitable and flew Kamm, along with representatives from *Newsweek* magazine and the American Broadcasting Corporation, to a relocation hamlet in Song My village where some My Lai 4 survivors were living.

The newsmen were given only one hour on the ground, and their interviews with the villagers were taped by a public information officer from the Americal Division. Kamm borrowed a typewriter, banged out a dispatch in which he quoted survivors as saying that 567 Vietnamese men, women and children were massacred by the Ameri-

cans, and telephoned it to the *Times'* Saigon bureau in time
for it to make page 1 of Monday's paper. Later Kamm tried
unsuccessfully to get interviews with U. S. Ambassador
Ellsworth Bunker and General Creighton Abrams, the
military commander for Vietnam. He did get to see a public
information officer in Saigon, who "treated me very coolly.
He apparently felt that I had ratted on our side."

Kamm's report was also treated coolly by the *Times'* main
competitor, the *Washington Post,* which chose to publish a
Pentagon statement describing Kamm's story as exaggerated. This denial was placed on page 16. Other newspapers were similarly skeptical about My Lai, and initially,
few commented editorially on the massacre.

The press was also cautious about Ron Ridenhour's role
in exposing the incident. Ben Cole of the *Arizona Republic,*
writing a day after other newspapers published the massacre
story, told about Ridenhour for the first time, and revealed
that the Pentagon had confirmed it was Ridenhour's letter
that had started the investigation. The AP picked up a few
lines of Cole's story, and one of its reporters in California
called Ridenhour for a brief interview. "Viet Slaying Tipster
Sees More Involved" was the headline a San Francisco
paper put over the subsequent wire service story.

I flew out to California on November 17 to interview
Ridenhour at Claremont College. No other newsman had
yet taken the trouble to visit him. Ridenhour, delighted
that his story had finally been made public, gave me a
copy of his original letter, and his subsequent correspond-
ence with the Army and Congress. Most important, he
also supplied me with the names and addresses of Michael
Terry and Michael Bernhardt. I left Ridenhour in the early
afternoon, drove back to Los Angeles International Airport
and took an evening flight to Salt Lake City. From there,
it was a ninety-minute drive over snowy mountain passes to

Orem, Utah, and to the home of Michael Terry. I knocked
at the door of the darkened house. A younger brother let
me in; he woke up Terry and the ex-GI came out to talk. I
told him who I was and what I wanted. He thought a second,
then asked, "Do you want me to tell you the same thing I
told Colonel Wilson?"

I got to Bernhardt at Fort Dix, New Jersey, the next
afternoon, came back to Washington, and wrote the second
Dispatch story based on the eyewitness accounts of My Lai
4 for newspapers of November 20. Another revelation about
that day was also in the works by that time.

On Tuesday, November 18, Joseph Eszterhas, a general
assignment reporter for the *Cleveland Plain Dealer,* received a phone call from an old schoolmate, an ex-GI
named Ron Haeberle, who said he had photographs of the
massacre. Haeberle had picked Eszterhas because the reporter had edited the newspaper at a school both had attended. Eszterhas was properly cautious: he conducted
hours of taped interviews with Haeberle at the newspaper's
office, trying to put together a full account of the photographer's involvement. And on the nineteenth he telephoned
the Pentagon, seeking confirmation that Haeberle was indeed at My Lai 4 on March 16, 1968. He did not get it
immediately. Later in the day Haeberle was called at home
by Captain Aubrey Daniels of Fort Benning, then directing the prosecution against Calley, and was asked not to
publish his pictures. Daniels warned that the photos would
"inflame public opinion" and might seriously jeopardize
the rights of Calley and the others. Haeberle told Eszterhas
about the call, and the reporter, still reluctant to release the
story without official confirmation of Haeberle's mission
that day, telephoned Fort Benning and received the same
warning that Haeberle got from Daniels. The *Plain Dealer*
now knew the photographs were authentic. The interview

with Haeberle—and some of his photographs, depicting slaughtered women and children—were published November 20, the same day my interviews quoting Bernhardt and Terry were made available.

The articles and photographs had an immediate shock effect in England, where the My Lai 4 massacre reports pushed news of the second U. S. landing on the moon off front pages on eight of Britain's nine morning newspapers. "The Story That Stunned America" headlined the conservative *Daily Mail*. The equally conservative *Daily Sketch,* in a front-page editorial, wrote that "the Americans were dragged down to the level of terrorism practiced by the Viet Cong. From today the Vietnam war is over . . . the President will have to pull out." The *Daily Sketch*'s main headline read: "War Crime. If This Can Happen, America Has Lost." Eyewitness accounts of the massacre were prominently displayed on page 1 of the influential *Times of London*. George Brown, former Foreign Secretary and a leader of Britain's ruling Labour Party, added to the furor when he told a radio audience that he wished Americans would "stop weeping and get on with winning the war." Thirty-two fellow members of the Labour Party demanded Brown's resignation, while others applauded his statement during bitter debate in the House of Commons. A group of demonstrators staged a noisy protest over My Lai 4 in front of the American Embassy; a memorial monument to President John F. Kennedy at Runnymede, England, was defaced by a Nazi swastika.

The reaction to the revelations about My Lai 4 in Great Britain was profound compared to that of the United States. In America, perhaps because of the less prominent newspaper coverage, the public was unable to comprehend the full significance of the incident. The impact of Haeberle's photographs and Bernhardt and Terry's eyewitness reports was partially diminished by the *Washington Post,* for example, in a story suggesting that the hardships suffered by Charlie Company might be responsible for its actions. "For Company C, in March, 1968," said one *Post* story, "the Pinkville rice paddies and battered hamlets were a nightmare of booby traps and mines." One Associated Press dispatch attempting to explain the atmosphere in Vietnam included the following in its fourth paragraph: "In Vietnam the killing of civilians was a practice established by the Viet Cong as a major part of the war long before the first U. S. ground troops were committed in March, 1965." The statement, though factual, was not relevant to what Charlie Company did on that March 16.

On November 25 the Army formally announced that Calley had been ordered to stand trial at a general court-martial for the premeditated murder of 109 Vietnamese civilians. Charges against Sergeant David Mitchell had been announced a few days earlier; he was accused of assaulting thirty Vietnamese civilians with intent to commit murder.

The newspapers continued being cautious. Most of them still refrained from commenting editorially. Air Force Lieutenant General (Retired) Ira C. Eaker, a conservative columnist on military affairs for the *Detroit News,* wrote how officers in Vietnam were bitter over what they saw as the press's failure to report Viet Cong atrocities. "I asked one of the Joint Chiefs of Staff why the Pentagon did not release any more Red atrocity stories," Eaker wrote on November 22. "He said it was against Administration policy, since this might build up a war psychology in the country which would pressure our leadership to use more force than it wanted to use in this limited conflict." Two days later, however, Army officers in Saigon made available "newly found" captured Viet Cong documents showing that Communist troops killed nearly 2,900 Vietnamese during

the Hue offensive in February, 1968. Officers said the documents went unnoticed in U. S. military files for nineteen
months until a correspondent's questions about Hue brought
them to light. "I know it sounds incredible, but that's the
truth," one official said.

As yet there was little investigative reporting on the
part of the American press to determine exactly what had
happened, perhaps because newspapers did not try to locate
former members of Charlie Company. By Friday, November 21, I had found Paul Meadlo in Terre Haute, Indiana.
Meadlo agreed to tell his story on television, and David
Obst and the Dispatch lawyers arranged to produce him—
for a fee—on the CBS evening news with Walter Cronkite.
His confession, later published in newspapers around the
world, stunned the nation. "Many of us sat in sheltered
living rooms," wrote columnists Richard Harwood and Laurence Stern of the *Washington Post,* "perhaps starting in on
a dinner martini as Meadlo's face showed on the screen.
. . . From the vantage point of those living rooms Meadlo
was the American 'gook'—the scapegoat and the buffer
between the torn bodies in open graves at My Lai and
ourselves." That Sunday the *Post* devoted three full pages
to the story.

The disclosure of the My Lai massacre cleared the way
for published accounts of previously witnessed American
atrocities in South Vietnam. Suddenly reporters were finding out that their newspapers were eager to print stories
about the shooting of civilians in Vietnam. On December 5,
1969, an AP reporter told of an incident he had witnessed
four years earlier: "Frustration and fear . . . were at work
on a group of American Marines I accompanied into a village south of Da Nang in 1965. A half squad, out of a
regimental-size force, went on a brief rampage, killing a

group hiding in a civilian air raid shelter. One marine called out, 'Whoosh, I'm a killer today. I got me two.' Another said, 'Kill them, I don't want anyone moving.' " Three days later another AP dispatch reported that "it was a rising storm of criticism from civilian province advisers against tough tactics by the U. S. Army's 9th Infantry Division that resulted in that unit being the first to go home when President Nixon decided on troop withdrawals. The 9th Division prided itself on killing 100 Viet Cong a day, every day. Civilian Americans in the provinces often complained to newsmen that innocent civilians were sometimes included in the totals." Both stories could have been written and published much earlier. But few reporters would have dared to file such copy, and few newspapers would have dared to publish it.

At the least, Meadlo's CBS appearance made the American press finally face up to the fact that something very terrible had indeed happened at My Lai 4. Newspapers across the country began making judgments about the massacre, and they were uniformly harsh. John S. Knight, president of the Knight newspaper chain, wrote that "the indiscriminate killings at Song My may now dramatize the larger question of why we remain in Vietnam." The *Philadelphia Inquirer* described My Lai 4 as "the kind of atrocity generally associated with the worst days of Hitler and Stalin and other cruel despotisms." The *Washington Star* noted that "when all is said, however, it is simply appalling to think of American soldiers gunning down helpless civilians, especially children and women, as the latter sought in vain to shield their offspring."

Even conservative columnists were no longer able to dismiss My Lai 4. Columnist Ray Cromley of the Newspaper Enterprise Association suggested in all seriousness that America could begin to repay its debt to the Vietnamese by "sending packages of those small things that poor Vietnamese villagers require to live. . . . We can make certain that doctors and surgeons are available to remedy so far as is possible the permanent disfigurement of survivors. . . . The Vietnamese people are a very humble people. They respond above all to men and women who accept personal responsibility. They live in a harsh world and know that terrible things happen. So they are amazingly forgiving when men and women personally show their desire to make friends."

Even after acknowledging the facts of My Lai 4, many conservative newspapers struggled to evade its implications. "Americans should not be deceived," wrote the *Chicago Tribune* on November 29, "by the contemptible lamentations that we are all guilty and that our troops in Viet Nam have been brutalized by the war and are just as inhuman as the Communists." The *National Observer,* after noting that the massacre stories could not be dismissed, added these words of protest: "It is not the 'system,' whatever its shortcomings, or the policy, whatever its failings, that are to blame. . . . The full story must be learned . . . and when it is learned, individual responsibility must be fixed."

The weekly magazines, however, did meet all of the issues squarely. Both *Newsweek* and *Time* magazines published cover stories on the massacre on the same Monday, each reporting extensively on the prejudice of GIs toward the Vietnamese. *Life* purchased the Haeberle photographs and reproduced many of them in color, along with an extensive eyewitness account of the incident. Ridenhour's status soared from a "tipster" to the *New York Times* "Man in the News."

Some military men, like Colonel Oran Henderson, former commander of the 11th Brigade, who was attending the Armed Forces Staff College at Norfolk, Virginia, still had their doubts about Ridenhour's motives. "I can't believe a guy who did not participate in something, that his conscience would bother him a year later more than the men involved," Henderson said. Something else troubled him more: "Up to about two weeks ago," he told a reporter on November 27, "I would have sworn, 'No, it [the massacre] could not have happened without my knowing about it.'" Now, he added, "I begin to wonder."

11

Vietnam Reacts

WHEN news of My Lai 4 broke out in America, President Nguyen Van Thieu of South Vietnam reacted the way he thought the U. S. military would appreciate: he ordered the Vietnamese newspapers not to print accounts of the massacre and arranged for an immediate denial to be issued to the world press.

The newspaper blackout in Vietnam lasted eight days. When it ended on November 21, the newspaper *Chinh Luan* (Right Opinion), one of the most influential in Saigon, published an interview with Foreign Minister Tran Van Lan, announcing that President Thieu had ordered an investigation. The results of the Thieu study were made public the next day by the South Vietnamese Defense Ministry; it said the accounts of a massacre by U. S. soldiers were "completely untrue."

Thieu's study was based on a confidential report given President Thieu by Major General Hoang

Xuan Lam, commander of the country's five northern provinces. The ministry said that Task Force Barker had made heavy contact with strong Communist forces inside My Lai 4. "The hamlet was organized as a fortified Viet Cong hamlet with bunkers and was under the administration of the Viet Cong," the report said. After heavy fighting, the bodies of 125 Viet Cong were found inside the area, along with twenty dead civilians who were killed by crossfire and by air and artillery strikes.

An American military spokesman in Saigon, asked about the discrepancy between the Saigon version of events and the fact of the U. S. Army's placement of charges against Lieutenant Calley, said, "I don't know that there is any discrepancy." A U. S. Embassy spokesman told newsmen that all statements on My Lai 4 would have to come from the Pentagon; at the Pentagon there was no immediate comment.

Thieu's report immediately set off another round of political infighting. Senator Tran Van Don, a leading opponent of Thieu who also served as chairman of the Senate Defense Committee, announced on November 25 that he would conduct his own investigation into the affair. He decried Thieu as "the valet of the Americans, who are his sole support." Later Senator Bui Van Giai, chairman of the Senate Interior Committee and a member of the Defense Committee, announced he would join Don in the inquiry.

The Vietnamese public, inured to atrocities after twenty-five years of civil war, began to take an interest—although many Saigon citizens were astonished to learn of the extensive shock in America over the My Lai 4 reports. On November 27 three Vietnamese newspapers published editorials praising the United States for its public discussion of the case and criticizing the Saigon regime's reticence to speak out. The independent *Chinh Luan* wrote: "If their own government should consider [the My Lai residents'] deaths as insignificant, although they died at the hands of those who presumably came here to save them, then this attitude is indeed one of sheer irresponsibility, denoting cowardice and worthy of contempt."

More than 700 Roman Catholics drove past the National Assembly building in Saigon to demonstrate in support of the Catholic Greater Union's demand for a full investigation into My Lai 4. Huyen Quang, a Buddhist leader, also insisted on an investigation. He announced that he had asked Buddhists in the My Lai area to provide him with a full report on the slayings, and described President Thieu's attitude as "shameful."

The growing discord prompted Vice-President Nguyen Cao Ky—the former Air Force Marshal who was a rival as well as a partner of President Thieu—to call for a re-examination of the incident. "We must investigate the whole matter so as to know exactly what has happened and how," Ky told newsmen on November 29. "We have instructed the Defense Ministry to reopen the investigation." Later, aides of the president denied that the investigation would begin again, and made clear that Ky had no constitutional power to order an investigation. Hoang Duc Nha, President Thieu's press secretary, said, "The case is definitely closed. There is not the least indication that it would be reopened."

By this time the antics of the South Vietnamese government over My Lai 4 were a source of growing embarrassment in Washington, as more and more former members of Charlie Company told their story in newspapers and on television in the United States.

On December 1 Senator Don tried to lead a group of senators and house members of the Vietnamese National Assembly from Quang Ngai City through rice paddies and dirt trails to My Lai 4. The group, heavily protected by troops and armored vehicles, never got there. When it was less than a mile away, some nearby U. S. marines suddenly fired warning shots, signaling that an enemy force was in the area. U. S. artillery shells began falling, and the legislators, although not totally convinced of the imminence of an enemy attack, left. They traveled instead to a fenced-in refugee camp in Song My, where some survivors of My Lai 4 had been resettled. There they were met by copies of a psychological-warfare poster depicting alleged Viet Cong atrocities in Quang Ngai. Newsmen later were told that the posters, produced by a joint United States–South Vietnamese unit, had been put in place a day earlier. Once in the village, the house and senate members were unable to find and interrogate any survivors, although newsmen recalled that they had no trouble finding these survivors on earlier trips. The province chief, Colonel Thon That Khien, and the Son Tinh district chief, Captain Tran Ngoc Tan, who earlier had verified aspects of the massacre to reporters, then proceeded to give the legislators a briefing in which they upheld the government's version on all points.

The frustrating day convinced Senator Don and the others that they would be better off without any government assistance. Don spent the next two days privately interrogating survivors and officials without troops or newsmen in attendance. Among those he visited was Do Tan Nhon, the hamlet chief of Tu Cung who was now living in Quang Ngai City. Don showed him the photographs in *Life* magazine, and was amazed when the hamlet chief picked out his wife, mother and daughter from among the crowd of women and children shown seconds before their murder. Nhon's daughter, Don said later, was the pretty girl that the GIs had molested. The senator reported on December 3 that many civilians in My Lai 4 had been killed by small-arms fire at close range. In a *New York Times* interview, Don also said that government officials had no idea how many civilians were killed in the hamlet because the American forces were not obligated to report such deaths. The senator also debunked the statements of Major General Lam, who had made the earlier report to President Thieu. "He knows nothing about it," Don said of General Lam, "but the government communiqué is based on his report." No South Vietnamese official seriously dealt with the massacre reports, Don complained, although the war was "systematically killing the population." The people of Vietnam, he added, "float between the Communists and the government, which does not protect them."

A similar analysis was also being prepared by members of the Vietnamese House of Representatives, who had joined the senators on the trip to the My Lai area. The house members told newsmen before filing their official report that they would say the number of victims in My Lai 4 was higher than announced by the government. Privately, many agreed that as many as 500 persons were killed by Americans that day—but in two hamlets.

The house investigators, who included four residents of the Quang Ngai area, explained they had evidence that many civilians also were slain by a different element of Task Force Barker at Co Luy village, two miles east of My Lai 4.* But the legislators said that they would not include

* Papers on file at the province district headquarters in Quang Ngai late in 1969 revealed that the Song My village chief testified that as many as 900 persons were killed in Co Luy by American GIs on March 16, 1968, as well as 450 to 500 in My Lai 4. The village chief's reports were sent in late March or early April, 1968, through channels to the Son Tinh district chief and then to the province headquarters, where they were noted in a statement dated April 14, 1968, and signed by U. S. Captain Angel M. Rodriguez, then assistant district adviser in Son Tinh. Rodriguez dismissed both My Lai and Co Luy reports as propaganda. None of the Charlie Company GIs interviewed mentioned any other killings that day.

their personal beliefs in the final report because of the great propaganda value it would have to the Viet Cong and North Vietnamese, and the damage it could do to United States–South Vietnamese relations.

When the senate and house reports finally were filed, they were inconclusive. In its summary made public December 15, Senator Don's committee would acknowledge only that a minimum of forty-three civilians had been slain by U. S. troops in My Lai 4. The committee explained the curious statistic by saying they had personally interviewed nine survivors of nine families, who specifically cited the loss of forty-three relatives. The House Defense Committee reported two days later, and refused to label the March 16 attack as a massacre. It did note, however, that the GIs "caused casualties and property damage beyond military needs."

The hedged reports failed to create a stir in Saigon, where the government still was insisting that there had been no massacre at My Lai 4. Senator Don, a former army general who helped to overthrow President Ngo Dinh Diem in the 1963 coup, brought up the subject again in early January, when the full senate acted on his committee's report. Don presented the forty-page report with a speech charging that President Thieu "must bear full responsibility for the incident" because the South Vietnamese government had failed to protect Song My. "The executive branch hid the truth and considered the case as closed," Don said. "By so doing it demeaned the people and the armed forces." After a five-hour debate, however, twenty-five of the twenty-nine senators present voted in support of a watered-down resolution describing the incident as "an isolated act by an American unit and not the policy of the United States armed forces." The resolution did not describe the killings in My Lai 4 as a massacre, and also did not assign any responsibility to President Thieu. The senate vote was a major victory for the president.

A few weeks later the Unified Buddhist Congregation of Vietnam reported that its study of My Lai 4 had determined that 394 civilians were killed, 176 missing, and 23 wounded. The Buddhists called on the Thieu government to "repent before the people" for its handling of the case. The report was given little press attention.

Officials at the U. S. Embassy in Saigon, of the U. S. military command and in Washington did not comment on the Buddhist report, nor did they comment on any of the earlier studies, reports and denials issued by President Thieu, Vice-President Ky, Senator Don and the other members of the democratic government of South Vietnam and its National Assembly.

12

America
Reacts

ON December 1, one week after Paul Meadlo's startling television confession, the *Wall Street Journal* published an informal poll on My Lai 4 that its reporters had taken in cities across the nation. The results were interesting. Many of those interviewed refused to believe that the mass killings had taken place; others wondered why the incident was attracting so much attention.

"It was good," exclaimed a fifty-five-year-old elevator starter in Boston. "What do they give soldiers bullets for—to put in their pockets?" In Cleveland a woman defended the shooting of children: "It sounds terrible to say we ought to kill kids, but many of our boys being killed over there are just kids, too." A Los Angeles salesman said, "I don't believe it actually happened. The story was planted by Viet Cong sympathizers and people inside this country who are trying to get us out of Vietnam sooner." A teletype inspector in Philadelphia also said he didn't think it happened: "I can't believe our boys' hearts are that rotten." Not all of the 200 persons interviewed had such extreme attitudes, but only a handful said that what happened at My Lai 4 had changed their minds on the war.

Much of America's anger at the disclosures was directed toward the newspapers and television stations publicizing them. The *Cleveland Plain Dealer,* on the morning it published Ron Haeberle's shocking photographs of My Lai 4, received more than 250 telephone calls. About 85 percent of them said that the photographs should not have been published. "Your paper is rotten and anti-American," one woman said. Another asked, "How can I explain these pictures to my children?" When one of the photographs, depicting about twenty slain women and children in a ditch, was later published on the front page of the *Washington Star,* that paper received calls complaining that the photograph was obscene. The callers were alluding to the fact that some of the dead victims were unclothed. After his interview with Meadlo, CBS correspondent Mike Wallace received 110 telephone calls, all but two of them abusive. One viewer fired off a telegram saying: "Wallace is pimping for the protesters." A *New York Times* survey of some GIs serving in the Quang Ngai area near My Lai 4 found wholesale resistance to the idea that Charlie Company had massacred some civilians. "There's gotta be something missing," one GI complained. Another said, "The company must have been hit hard before the action."

In early December, American Legion members in Columbus, Georgia, home of Fort Benning, took a four-column newspaper advertisement in the local newspaper proclaiming support for Calley and Captain Medina. The advertisement accused newspapers and television of trying to "tear down America and its armed forces." A week later a group of former servicemen in Atlanta, Georgia, began a petition movement to get the Army to drop its charges against Calley. During a rally on December 14, James A. Smith, chief spokesman for the group, said that "no American would ever kill 109 people like that" and suggested that the Haeberle photographs were fake. About fifty to seventy-five persons attended the rally, far less than the two hundred expected, but Smith said his group had collected 3,000 signatures on the petition. A few days later Calley personally opened a bank account with the Fourth National Bank of Columbus to handle contributions to his defense. Within a month the bank received several hundred letters, and more than $1,200 was on deposit. Calley had by then reached the status of a celebrity in Columbus. Most of the citizens openly supported him; some used-car salesmen even put his name in lights in front of their lots, urging contributions to the Calley Defense Fund.

A statewide poll published shortly before Christmas by the *Minneapolis Tribune* showed that 49 percent of 600 persons interviewed there believed that the reports of mass murder at My Lai 4 were false. To another query, 43 percent said they were horrified when they first heard the story and decided that it wasn't true. A later *Time* magazine poll of 1,600 households indicated that 65 percent of the American public believed such incidents were bound to happen in any war; and an even greater percent of the public, asked about news media coverage, complained that the press and TV should not have reported statements by GIs prior to a court-martial. The Pentagon even produced a poll. Deputy Secretary of Defense David Packard showed a group of newsmen a public-opinion study which he said had been conducted in the upper half of South Vietnam, an area that includes Quang Ngai Province. It showed, Packard said, that "only 2.8 percent of the people disapprove of the behavior of American troops in their country."

By mid-January six American Legion posts in Jacksonville, Florida, announced plans to raise a $200,000 defense
fund for Calley. The lieutenant was granted permission to
leave Fort Benning and fly to Jacksonville for a fund-raising
party. He was greeted like a hero. A few fellow passengers
recognized him, tapped him on the shoulder as they
climbed off the airliner and said, "Good luck, son." A newspaper poll of the citizens in Duval County (Jacksonville)
showed that more than 71 percent thought the Army should
drop its charges against Calley. Robert C. Lenten, commander of one of the local Legion posts, told newsmen,
"We are not saying he is guilty or not guilty. We feel Lieutenant Calley has been condemned and vilified for performance of his duties in combat without benefit of the opportunity to defend himself." In February former Governor
George Wallace of Alabama endorsed Calley publicly. They
met for more than one hour in Montgomery, Alabama, on
February 20, and then came out together to face a battery
of reporters. Wallace said he was "proud" to meet Calley
and added, "I'm sorry to see the man tried. They ought to
spend the time trying folks who are trying to destroy this
country instead of trying those who are serving their country." The 1968 Presidential aspirant said, "I've been shot
at myself and there's nothing like it." Calley said little.

At Fort Benning, many of Calley's fellow officers were
outraged by the murder charges. "They're using this as a
goddamned example," one officer said. "He's a good soldier.
He followed orders." Another said, "It could happen to any
of us. He's killed and seen a lot of killing . . . killing be-
comes nothing in Vietnam. He knew that there were civilians there, but he also knew that there were VC among
them." A third officer, a West Point graduate, added,
"There's this question—I think anyone who goes to Nam

asks it. What's a civilian? Someone who works for us at day and puts on Viet Cong pajamas at night?"

One veteran of Vietnam told his local newspaper, in the aftermath of the My Lai 4 controversy, how he had witnessed Viet Cong prisoners' being thrown out of helicopters during interrogation by U. S. GIs. He was quickly subjected to a barrage of abusive telephone calls. "You ought to take a helicopter ride with me," one man said. "I know just exactly what to do with guys like you. You should be the one taken up and dropped out." Another caller said, "Someone should burn your house down, and maybe they just will."

Protests were voiced also by the Hawks in Congress. Senator Allen Ellender, Louisiana Democrat, told a television interviewer that the Vietnamese who had been slain "got just what they deserved." Senator Ernest Hollings, South Carolina Democrat, publicly wondered if all soldiers who made "a mistake in judgment" were going to be tried "as common criminals, as murderers."

Senator Peter H. Dominick, Colorado Republican, led a number of legislators in attacks on the reporters who disseminated the news about My Lai 4, repeatedly accusing the news media of sensationalism and trial by press. In doing so, he singled out the interview with Meadlo and the publication in *Life* magazine of Haeberle's photographs. "They go too far," Dominick told the Senate on December 2, "when interviews of potential witnesses are carried on nationwide TV, when these interviews are republished in newspapers all across the country over and over, and when a nationwide magazine publishes photographs of a highly inflammatory, and, I might add, revolting nature . . ." He argued that the public's right to know was met in full by the Army's public release of the charges against Calley on September 6.

In the House, a number of conservative legislators attacked Dispatch News Service for its role in the My Lai 4 revelation. Representative Ed Foreman, New Mexico Republican, asked, "Why have not these money-hungry headline-writing sensationalists written about the brutal Communist murder of thousands of innocent victims—men, women, children and babies—in South Vietnam, in Hungary, in Czechoslovakia and elsewhere . . . ?" John R. Rarick, Louisiana Democrat, consistently described My Lai 4 as the "massacre hoax," and warned, "The American people are daily becoming more aware that the news media is being used as a weapon of psychological warfare against them." Lawrence J. Hogan, Maryland Republican, placed into the *Congressional Record* a letter he received from a Vietnam veteran, saying in part: "It is probable you learned enough about the Oriental mind to find nothing incongruous about a Viet Cong woman advancing with a submachine gun on U. S. troops with her baby in her arms. These people are not stupid. They have our number very well. . . . They know our reverence for soft women and helpless children and know how to capitalize on this strictly Judeo-Christian hangup. Caucasians simply can't fight these people according to western precepts and the grunts in the field learn this often after they have been half wiped out."

On December 9, nearly a month after the initial disclosures, Representative Richard H. Ichord, chairman of the House Committee on Internal Security, gave a public screening of photographs of Hue to put the My Lai massacre in "proper perspective." He complained to the audience of seventy-five—in a Congressional hearing room prepared for 300 spectators—that the world press was giving wider coverage to My Lai 4 "where the alleged acts of individuals are in violation of official regulations" than to the "systematic" murder of civilians in Hue and elsewhere in Vietnam by the Viet Cong.

The following thirty-minute slide show prepared by the Defense Department included only two photographs of victims of the Hue massacre, although there were many other pictures showing maps, diagrams of graveyards, Viet Cong propaganda quotations (displayed against a pink background with a superimposed red hammer and sickle) and photos of atrocities from elsewhere in Vietnam. "Don't you have any more photos of atrocities in Hue?" Ichord, a Democrat from Missouri, asked the lieutenant colonel giving the briefing. The officer said no, and a high-ranking Pentagon official later confirmed that he hadn't seen more than a few altogether.

Congressional activities reached a high point on December 15, when Chairman L. Mendel Rivers, of the Armed Services Committee, joined by 140 other supporters of the Vietnam war, pushed through a House resolution praising "each serviceman and veteran of Vietnam for his individual sacrifice, bravery, dedication, initiative, devotion to duty . . ." In so doing, the House overrode a complaint by Representative Jonathan Bingham, New York Democrat, that the praise of "each" serviceman "was unfortunate, especially at the present time when we are so concerned about the apparent massacre at My Lai."

There was an equally strong denunciation by Senator George S. McGovern, the liberal South Dakota Democrat, who told a television interviewer on November 30 that "what this incident has done is to tear the mask off the war. . . . I think that for the first time millions of Americans are realizing that we have stumbled into a conflict where we not only of necessity commit horrible atrocities against the people of Vietnam, but where in a sense we brutalize our own people and our own nation. I think it's more than Lieutenant Calley involved here. I think a national policy is on trial."

But few other Dove voices were heard discussing My Lai 4 in the Senate or House during the weeks following the first reports; apparently the liberal legislators sensed what the subsequent polls showed—that many Americans were ignoring or dismissing the implications of what happened there. Others were just as astute; it took President Nixon twenty-five days to make his first public statement about the massacre.

The Administration's over-all response to the matter was marked by caution. The first public statement was issued jointly November 19 by the U. S. Embassy and military command in Saigon, and almost routinely expressed disapproval of the massacre: "The United States government does not condone atrocities in any way, at any time, under any conditions." Five days later the Pentagon emphasized that the Nixon Administration did not learn of the incident until the Ridenhour letter reached Washington. A spokesman for Secretary of Defense Melvin A. Laird told newsmen that "Secretary Laird personally learned of this matter shortly after he assumed office." At the same time this public disclaimer was being made, Laird privately expressed his feelings in much stronger terms. He sent a letter to Senator J. W. Fulbright, chairman of the Foreign Relations Committee, saying he was "shocked and sick" when he first learned of the massacre. "I want to make clear, Mr. Chairman," Laird wrote, "that the Nixon Administration is determined to insure absolute compliance with our orders and with the laws of war." A few days later both General Harold Johnson, who was Army Chief of Staff in 1968, and General William C. Westmoreland, who was then commander of military forces in Saigon, also disavowed any immediate knowledge of the incident.

On November 26, two days after Meadlo's TV appearance, Army Secretary Stanley R. Resor showed some of Haeberle's photographs to members of the Senate Armed Services Committee at a special briefing in the Capitol. In an accompanying statement, Resor attempted to explain that what happened at My Lai 4 was an isolated occurrence: "I have reviewed what we know of the incident at My Lai with a number of officers who have served in Vietnam. It is their judgment—a judgment which I personally endorse and share—that what apparently occurred at My Lai is wholly unrepresentative of the manner in which our forces conduct military operations in Vietnam. . . . I am convinced that their over-all record is one of decency, consideration and restraint toward the unfortunate civilians who find themselves in a zone of military operations."

The pictures, however, shocked most senators. Daniel K. Inouye, a Hawaii Democrat who lost an arm while serving in World War II, left the hearing room and said, "Having been in combat myself, I thought I would be hardened, but I must say I am a bit sickened." Haeberle's photographs were also shown to the House Armed Services Committee. Afterward Representative Leslie C. Arends, Illinois Republican, told newsmen, "The pictures were pretty gruesome. That's why I walked out. I have one of those queasy stomachs." The tone, however, was set by Chairman John C. Stennis of the Armed Services Committee, who issued a statement after the Resor slide show, saying that My Lai is "indeed a shocking affair . . . it should also be noted that this incident was contrary to every rule and instruction the Army has issued in connection with the conduct of the South Vietnamese operation."

Only Senator Stephen C. Young, an elderly Democratic maverick from Ohio who served on the Armed Services Committee, publicly expressed any kind of compassion for the victims: "It's really terrifying and horrible, looking at a Vietnam woman—a young woman—standing up and begging, with young people all about her, and knowing that she would be killed an instant later by American bullets. No one can question there was an atrocious slaughter of from two hundred to three hundred civilians."

The White House was under intense pressure to react in some manner. Press and public reaction had become increasingly critical throughout Europe and Asia; the shocked reaction to the news of the events at My Lai 4 initially expressed in Britain seemed to be spreading throughout the world. One State Department official told a newsman that cables from U. S. embassies everywhere indicated "revulsion" over My Lai. "It's setting back United States policy everywhere." The State Department finally asked the President in late November to take a personal role in decrying the incident.

On November 25 the White House unexpectedly announced that the United States would give up the use— even in retaliation—of biological weapons. "Mankind already carries in its own hands too many of the seeds of its own destruction," President Nixon said. "By the example we set today, we hope to contribute to an atmosphere of peace and understanding between all nations." Nixon acted only two weeks after the National Security Council had staged a full-fledged debate on the matter. Administration sources described it as an unusually quick response on matters so important. Some officials privately noted that a study of biological warfare and its effectiveness had been initiated in 1963 by the Arms Control and Disarmament Agency (ACDA). No responsible Administration official denied later that one reason for Nixon's haste was the growing furor over My Lai.

There was a sense of embarrassment, perhaps, in the White House. Just ten days before the story of My Lai 4 first was made public, President Nixon had sharply warned against Communist atrocities if the United States pulled out of Vietnam too soon. In a national television speech on November 3, the President had said: "We saw the prelude of what would happen in South Vietnam when the Communists entered the city of Hue last year. During their brief rule there, there was a bloody reign of terror in which 3,000 civilians were clubbed, shot to death and buried in mass graves."

The White House's initial response came on November 26, the same day Resor gave the showing on Capitol Hill. Press Secretary Ronald L. Ziegler in a statement took pains not only to depict My Lai 4 as an unfortunate aberration, but also to absolve the Nixon Administration from any responsibility. "All questions should be addressed to the Department of Defense," Ziegler said, "but I will give you this information: The alleged incident took place some ten months before this Administration came into office . . ." He deplored the incident as a "direct violation of United States military policy," and added that it "is abhorrent to the conscience of all the American people."

The White House became quiet again and the military began doing its best to keep potential witnesses from speaking out. The trial judge in the Calley case, Lieutenant Colonel Reid W. Kennedy, issued an order shortly after Meadlo's CBS appearance, telling all potential witnesses "to refrain from discussing with or disclosing to anyone . . . any information or evidence you may possess concerning the events that occurred on or about 16 March 1968. . . ." The prosecution and the defense, anxious to limit the damage to both the Army and to Calley's chances for a fair trial, asked the judge to make the bar apply to the press as well—but Kennedy refused.

Many members of Charlie Company simply ignored the attempted ban on talking, and their interviews continued to dominate the press in late November. Most of the ex-GIs assumed, apparently, that the Army no longer had any jurisdiction over them—an opinion reinforced by a 1955 United States Supreme Court declaration that military courts cannot try former members of the armed forces "no matter how intimate the connection between the offense and the concerns of military discipline." * As the interviews continued to appear, however, Pentagon correspondents were fed information pointing out that the Army was doing everything possible to get jurisdiction over former Charlie Company members in order to prosecute some of them for murder. On November 27 the *Washington Post* reported that the Pentagon was considering the establishment of a special military war-crimes tribunal to try the former GIs. On the next day an AP dispatch said essentially the same thing, but added that two never-before-invoked sections of the Military Code of Justice might have to be tested in order to gain this jurisdiction. Essentially the same approach was taken by Charles W. Corddry of the *Baltimore Sun* on November 28: "Army Studies How to Try My Lai Ex-GIs." The *Washington Star* reported on December 3 that the Army was planning to send the Justice Department a document outlining possible ways of trying ex-servicemen.

The Pentagon's sudden talk of war-crimes tribunals and the like paralleled an unsuccessful plea by both defense and prosecution in the Calley court-martial to get the Military Court of Appeals to bar news media from publishing any further interviews with participants in or wit-

* The case is *Toth vs. Quarles.*

nesses to the My Lai massacre. The plea was filed with the cooperation of the trial military judge, Lieutenant Colonel Kennedy. During a closed session at Fort Benning on November 28, three days after the attempt to restrain witnesses from speaking out, the judge agreed that his order was being violated, and suggested that the prosecution and defense seek redress from the Court of Military Appeals. In essence, Kennedy was acknowledging that he had no power to enforce the ban he had ordered. The Court of Military Appeals also had no real choice in the matter, since it lacked jurisdiction over news media. Without getting into the issue of jurisdiction, it ruled on December 2 —the day after the plea was made—that "determining the propriety and accuracy of the news stories they disseminate is the responsibility of the publisher" and not of a military court. The two military lawyers, Captain Aubrey Daniels, for the prosecution, and Major Kenneth A. Raby, military counsel for Calley, reportedly considered seeking an injunction from the Supreme Court to block future publicity, but were advised that they would first have to take their plea to lower federal courts.

These legal maneuverings over publicity were reported without comment by the nation's press, although it was still extremely unclear whether the basic goal of the Kennedy court was to protect the Army from further adverse publicity or to protect Lieutenant Calley's rights.

One clue, perhaps, came on December 3, when Lieutenant Colonel Kennedy made an exception to his rule barring potential witnesses from speaking and permitted the highest-ranking officer in Charlie Company, Captain Ernest Medina, to hold a news conference in the Pentagon the next day. Medina was accompanied by his lawyer, F. Lee Bailey of Boston, and explained his decision to speak: "I think the news media have been very biased and unfair, not only to myself, but to any other soldier in uniform; to the United States Army. Now they're making accusations, taking statements from individuals and the press . . . [and] not recording the other side of it. It's not fair to the other people that have served their country honorably, the people that are in uniform, and it's not fair to the soldiers that we have in Vietnam right now." Medina took advantage of the occasion to deny seeing his men shoot even one civilian that day, and also said he saw no evidence of a massacre. Some of those who had been speaking out against him and the company, he said, had been disciplinary problems in Vietnam. He then had this exchange with a reporter:

"Did the individuals make any money out of it [the interviews], as far as you know?"

"Oh . . . I'm not saying they did. I'm saying this might be one of the reasons. Another reason, I imagine, is that there are probably certain dissident groups in the United States that have probably welcomed the chance to talk to these people and get them to voice their opinion probably against the military, which, I imagine, a lot of them particularly did not care for."

Another reporter then broke in and asked the captain, "How do you explain the fact that an Army investigation has been under way since April, and that in August it was decided that charges would be brought? . . . That was not the press . . . it was Army investigators."

Bailey did not permit Medina to answer the question, which concluded the news conference. But, over all, Medina's performance was impressive; he spoke firmly and with confidence. He repeated his statements in a subsequent television appearance and in newspaper interviews that took up the next four or five days. No immediate attempt was made by the military court to bar him from speaking out, even after he repeatedly—and in public—denied issuing any orders to destroy the village, a claim that bore heavily on the defense of Lieutenant Calley and other suspects. Later Lieutenant Colonel Kennedy explained that he had excepted Medina from his order, "because I didn't think he would grant an interview." He then ordered Medina to stop talking.

On December 8 President Nixon told a news conference —his first since the massacre became known—that: "What appears was certainly a massacre, under no circumstances was it justified. . . . We cannot ever condone or use atrocities against civilians" to achieve the United States' goal of preventing the Vietnamese people from "having imposed upon them a government which has atrocity against civilians as one of its policies." The President also attempted to minimize the incident, but was much more circumspect about it than the men in the Pentagon: "I believe that it is an isolated incident. Certainly within this Administration we are doing everything possible to find out whether it was isolated. . . ."

Strictly speaking, even Nixon's words violated the military court's previously established pretrial publicity guidelines. On December 16 Colonel Kennedy took a final step to stop the media from continuing to cover the story. He asked the Justice Department to investigate four news organizations—including the Associated Press and the National Broadcasting Company—and three ex-GIs, among them Herbert Carter, for their roles in proliferating publicity about My Lai 4. Kennedy said his court had done "everything in its power" to curb this pretrial publicity. His actions received wide press attention at the time, although three months later there was no evidence of any subsequent action by the Justice Department.

There were many lawyers in Washington who thought the military court's actions lacked jurisdiction and constitutionality from the start, and were part of a Defense Department attempt to inhibit potential witnesses. For example, someone in the Pentagon provided *The New York Times* with a five-page directive outlining the proper response for violations of the Geneva Convention. The directive, issued to all military units in Vietnam on April 27, 1967, according to the *Times,* required every soldier witnessing or even hearing of a possible war crime to inform his commanding officer without delay. Publication of the order in the *Times* frightened many ex-Charlie Company GIs, even those who did not participate in the indiscriminate shooting of civilians that day. Some thought they could be held liable even at this late date for not informing the proper authority immediately after the incident.

A few days later Laird added to their concerns when he told a nationwide television audience that any present or former GI found to have any connection with the My Lai 4 massacre would be brought to trial. "If the investigations warrant a charge," he said, "the charges will be made." Yet more than two months later Pentagon officials were still telling inquiring newsmen that no decision had been made on the prosecution of former servicemen.

The only public figure to comment critically during this period on the military's apparent attempt to shut off further interviews was Senator Young, a former military judge. In a series of Senate speeches, Young vigorously attacked Judge Kennedy for his attempts to stop publicity: "Officials of the news media and all lawyers of course know the absurdity of the arrogant claims being made by this puffed-up lieutenant colonel with an obviously inflated ego. . . . Young men such as Paul Meadlo and other soldiers who were in My Lai . . . should know that Pentagon officials and this Lieutenant Colonel Kennedy have no authority whatever over them." The senator also criticized the Department of Defense for indicating that it had, or would have, jurisdiction over the ex-GIs. "All these former soldiers now in civilian life are definitely immune from prosecution for their part in the My Lai massacre," he told his colleagues. "I take a dim view of the Pentagon permitting statements to be made that charges will be instituted against these men."

Lieutenant Colonel Kennedy's order did not in any way or manner inhibit the defense counsel, George W. Latimer of Salt Lake City, from continuing to speak out on the case. And although the court eventually barred Medina from speaking out in public, his attorney, F. Lee Bailey, continued to take his case to the people. For example, within two days in mid-January, Bailey appeared on two Washington television shows. He told one interviewer on January 12 that as far as he was concerned, the accusations about a massacre at My Lai 4 were "a gross exaggeration until I see something more convincing than I have so far." On the next day he said he didn't think any one "of any higher rank than Lieutenant Calley is going to be put on trial because right above him is Captain Medina. . . . It wouldn't make it more fair to charge Medina if he had nothing to do with it. If Calley shot some people he shouldn't have shot . . . Medina didn't know about it, didn't tell him to, and had no opportunity to stop him."

The question of pretrial publicity relating to the rights of the accused was further confused by an abortive three-day hearing on My Lai 4 conducted by a House Armed Services Subcommittee headed by L. Mendel Rivers. The congressman marked the first day of testimony, December 9, by telling newsmen afterward that he was not yet ready to say that a massacre did indeed take place. On the next day the fourteen members of his special investigating subcommittee listened in stunned silence as Warrant Officer Hugh

Thompson outlined his story of that March 16. The pilot told how he had landed his helicopter in an attempt to rescue the Vietnamese civilians from a bunker and how he had ordered his two crewmen to train their guns on Calley and his men, and to fire on them if they tried to block the rescue of those civilians. Under hostile questioning from subcommittee members, most of them pro-military, Thompson told a slightly different story from the one he had provided Colonel Wilson the previous June. He said he had had another reason for having his men aim their guns at the American GIs: to ensure that no Viet Cong could sneak up behind the group and attack. Varying versions of his testimony were leaked to reporters afterward. "He got a little cute," one source said later. Most members of the committee were shocked by what the pilot reported. But not Rivers, apparently. He left the hearing room and announced to the waiting newsmen that Thompson "gave us no information to lead us to believe that anyone committed a massacre at My Lai." Committee members, strictly forbidden by Rivers to talk to reporters, were astounded and enraged by his statement. "I don't know how he could say that," one said in amazement.

Captain Medina testified before the committee on the next—and last—day of hearings. Medina praised his former superior, Lieutenant Colonel Frank Barker, head of Task Force Barker. "I'm sure he believed that there was no incident of war crimes or atrocities committed at My Lai 4, and I asked to make this statement on behalf of Mrs. Barker. . . . He was an outstanding task force commander, an outstanding soldier." At this point, according to witnesses, the committee jumped up and applauded the captain. Later Medina praised the "outstanding committee that is headed by Chairman Rivers" to newsmen, but refused to comment on his three hours of testimony. On the next day

Defense Secretary Laird convinced Rivers to call off the hearings.

A number of high Defense officials were furious at the Congressional squabbling over Thompson's testimony, but even more aggravating to them was Rivers' assertion that he had not yet received any evidence of a massacre. "If he'd read those papers on his desk, he'd know what went on," one official complained later. Rivers, needing to save face, announced later that he had named a select four-man panel, headed by Representative F. Edward Herbert, Louisiana Democrat, to continue a more deliberate, and secret, investigation into the whole affair.

The question of just who, or what agency, should investigate My Lai 4 was a dominant one for those liberals in the House and Senate who chose to speak out. Much of the early Congressional comment about the matter had come from the Hawks. Liberal legislators tended to avoid the issue, many saying privately that it could best be handled by supporters of the war, who would be hard-pressed to explain it away. Even those Doves who did speak of the larger implications of My Lai 4 tended to discuss them in terms of what issues a future investigation should raise. Senator Charles E. Goodell, a New York Republican and a leading critic of the Vietnam war, was among the first to decry the massacre, and called on Senator John C. Stennis of the Armed Services Committee to conduct an investigation. "Such barbarous treatment of Vietnamese civilians can totally destroy any credibility the United States can claim to have for its presence in Vietnam," Goodell said on November 20. Representative William L. Minshall, Ohio Republican, suggested that the House Appropriations Committee study the event. *The New York Times* and New York *News,* two newspapers of totally different philosophy, both suggested within a few days of each other that some group in Congress should take over the investigation of the massacre.

A number of prominent Americans also called for an independent probe of the events at My Lai 4. Senator Stennis, responding in effect to demands that his committee make an investigation, told a television interviewer that the panel should instead be composed of persons "outside the government and outside the military." Former Vice-President Hubert H. Humphrey suggested that a group, similar to the Warren Commission, be constituted by President Nixon. Former Supreme Court Justice Arthur J. Goldberg and a group of former State Department officials called for an investigation of "unquestionable impartiality" and suggested that President Nixon initiate one. The American Civil Liberties Union, in a statement urging that Calley be freed because of pretrial publicity, also recommended that a "public commission supported by public funds but independent of both the armed services and the Administration" be set up. Joseph Kraft, the liberal columnist, wrote that a commission selected by the Secretary of the Army and composed of distinguished civilian and military officials could accomplish "what the country most needs out of My Lai— that is, a reform of the Army by the Army." William S. White, the conservative columnist, endorsed the Stennis proposal for an impartial and unpolitical inquiry by an outside panel. "A good many people will not readily accept the findings of the court-martial," White warned.

For all of their efforts, calls and pleas, the distinguished group of legislators, former government officials, organizations and journalists ended up getting a closed-door investigation inside the Pentagon headed by a three-star general. There were no public complaints over that fact, nor was there any comment on the timing of the Pentagon's move— it came eleven days after the world first learned of the tragedy at My Lai 4.

13

The Peers Panel

ON November 24, almost seven months after the Ridenhour letter first reached the Pentagon, a decision was made to try to find out why, in essence, that young GI had learned what Colonel Henderson and other staff officers of the 11th Brigade had not. Army Secretary Resor and General Westmoreland announced that they had appointed Lieutenant General William R. Peers to head a panel and explore "the nature and scope" of the original Army investigations. The officials issued a joint directive to Peers, telling him that his study "will include a determination of the adequacy of the investigations or inquiries on this subject, their subsequent reviews and reports within the chain of command, and possible suppression or withholding of information by persons involved in the incident."

Peers, fifty-three, had worked for the Central Intelligence Agency during his career and was widely admired in the Army as a tough, blunt general; he had now drawn an almost impossible task: to determine if high-ranking career Army men had whitewashed an atrocity. "He'll be damned if he does and damned if he doesn't," one colleague said. From the Army's point of view, Peers had another qualification: he was not a West Point graduate, or "ringknocker"—the military's way of referring to graduates of the military academy who invariably wear their class rings. He would thus view men such as Major General Samuel Koster simply as fellow officers and not as fellow classmates. Adding to the sensitivity of Peers' investigation was the fact that Koster's post-American Division job was Superintendent of West Point, one of the most prestigious assignments in the military. Westmoreland himself had served in the same position en route to becoming Chief of Staff.

To the military men, then, Peers' appointment was eminently suitable. To former State Department pacification officials, however, his selection brought widespread dismay. They recalled Peers' insensitivity to the problems of civilians during a year as commander of the 4th U. S. Division in Vietnam. A number of former civilian Vietnam officials cited, as one example, Peers' disruption of a non-Viet Cong village in Pleiku and the subsequent forced resettlement of its 8,000 residents in early 1968. Peers had turned the village area into another free-fire zone. His plan was vigorously opposed by nearly every State Department pacification worker in Vietnam, including Ambassador Robert W. Komer, then the deputy for pacification to the U. S. Command in Saigon. Peers, citing a military need for the project, overruled the civilian advisers and resettled the villagers—who were Montagnards—in a new camp known as Ednap Enang. "I'm sure the general was well-meaning," one former State Department official said. "He wanted to move them from their huts to a new village with nice

straight streets, and houses with roofs." The uprooting co-
incided with the harvest season, and many of the civilians
were leaving the resettlement camp to return to their village,
which by then had been leveled by United States planes.
South Vietnamese troops eventually had to be sent in to
drive the villagers from the desolated area.

Former Ambassador Komer acknowledged in an interview that he had vigorously disagreed with the general
about the resettlement of the Montagnards. Komer added,
however, that he rated Peers "very, very high. I would say
he was one of the most sensitive and scientific of the commanders in Vietnam."

Peers began his review by summoning command officers of the 11th Brigade and the Americal Division to his
conference room deep in the basement of the Pentagon.
General Koster spent two long days testifying before the
Panel in mid-December. Peers and his hand-picked staff,
which included Colonel Wilson of the Inspector General's
office, then began systematically interrogating the members
of Charlie Company. Peers specifically had been told by
Resor and Westmoreland that "the scope of your investigation does not include, nor will it interfere with, ongoing
criminal investigations in progress." But it was clear from
the outset that he would, in fact, review exactly what did
happen on March 16. Liaison was immediately arranged
with the C.I.D. for the orderly transfer of evidence regarding that day, and the Army called in two private New York
attorneys, Robert MacCrate and Jerome K. Walsh, Jr., to
help. "We have to examine the facts and provide assurance
that this kind of thing doesn't happen again," MacCrate
told newsmen. "What we are engaged in is getting at the
facts—and we will get at the facts," the lawyer added. Beyond that statement, little else was said publicly about the
workings of the Panel.

When the investigation first began, newsmen were told it was closed to the public to avoid prejudicing the rights of those accused in the case, but those witnesses who appeared would be free to tell newsmen about their testimony. Officials assured reporters, however, that every effort would be made to tell them what was going on—but the only information released was a daily listing of witnesses before the Panel and an occasional advance notice of a field trip. By early March, when the Panel concluded its hearings, 398 witnesses had testified in secret, and only one of them had chosen to appear before the press. That was Captain Medina at his early-December news conference. The Army's explanation was that none of the other witnesses chose to appear before the public after testifying. Many Pentagon reporters felt, however, that the Army was discouraging any talk about testimony.

John A. Kesler of Terre Haute, Indiana, a lawyer for Paul Meadlo, provided the Army with a good reason—if it needed one—for considering censorship. Kesler accompanied Meadlo to his session before the Peers Panel on January 5, 1970, and later told newsmen that "I don't even know for sure what a massacre is, or an atrocity. That war over there is just a series of massacres every day, one after the other, and I can't conceive that privates in the Army can be held responsible for things the U. S. Army compels them to do when it takes them over there." Meadlo, Kesler said, "was taken into the Army by the draft when he didn't want to be there. . . . He has done nothing more than any soldier who was brought to Vietnam." Kesler's remarks were widely distributed over television and in the newspapers, in part because of the worldwide interest over Meadlo and his confession, but also because it was the first news to be generated from the Peers Panel since the Medina appearance.

The Panel itself was handicapped by an unclear legal status; it could not subpoena witnesses nor could it in any other way compel them to appear or to testify. Perhaps because of this, its members initially tried to provoke witnesses, even those no longer in the service, by pointing out their failure to uphold military law. Ex-combat correspondent Jay Roberts testified on December 17, and clashed repeatedly with the three-star general. "Peers read me all the regulations and said that I was supposed to go through the chain of command and report what I saw," Roberts said in an interview one day after his appearance. "He kept on asking me why I didn't do it, why I didn't ask Medina to stop." Roberts thought the line of questioning was naïve: "I wasn't going to go up to Medina that day. No, sir."

He and the general then got into an argument over the burning of homes by Charlie Company. "General Peers said it's never done in Vietnam without the permission of the South Vietnamese," the youth reported. "I just told him it was standard operating procedure to eliminate the enemy's shelter and his food supply." Roberts couldn't believe the apparent insulation of the general. "He kept on getting righteous. He gave me a speech that sounded like it could be almost word for word from any Army manual.

"Hell," the ex-GI said, shaking his head, "my eyebrows are longer than his hair." Roberts was the antithesis of a GI in appearance, with a handlebar mustache and stylishly long hair. He had been out of the Army for a year by then, and out of work, also. "We just didn't get along. I came in there and shook my hair down over my eyes. . . . I don't know what they [the officers] thought, but the enlisted man taking dictation was really grooving over it." But despite the difference in dress and other ways—or perhaps because of it—Roberts was a cooperative witness.

By January, Peers and his men were showing witnesses a

large map of My Lai 4 tracing the path of Medina. The purpose was to determine, apparently, how many bodies Medina
should have seen if he did in fact walk the route he claimed
through the village. Michael Bernhardt said that when he
testified in late January, "They had his route all plotted out
on the map."

Bernhardt, too, was a cooperative witness, although he
had his troubles with the Panel, which seemed openly hostile
to him as a member of Charlie Company. "I aggravated the
shit out of them," Bernhardt recalled. "They kept on saying,
'I'm a little amazed that you can't remember any better
than that. How long have you been a sergeant?' and things
like that. You know, they were leading me with questions
and everything. I think they're trying to drill us—they want
to convict these guys so then they can say, 'Well, we did it.' "

Bernhardt was particularly nonplused by a question asked
by Bland West, a civilian attorney for the Army who was
one of Peers' deputies. "He asked me if I knew that it was
my brigade policy to fire two shots at a Vietnamese and then
shoot if they don't stop. I told them that I didn't know about
it, but it seemed unreasonable to me because if I was those
people I wouldn't stop for anything, especially after My
Lai 4."

The Panel's aggressive interrogation approach had no effect on some witnesses. But there were other factors that
made some ex-GIs talk: fear, shame, a desire to help the
Army. Sometimes it was because of a chance meeting. John
Smail, summoned from his home in Renton, Washington, to
the Pentagon, was determined not to name any names. He,
like other witnesses, spent the night at a nearby motel in
Virginia in rooms reserved by the Army. Before his appearance he ran into another former member of Charlie
Company, who told him that the Peers group had incriminating evidence on many of the men. Smail became so

angry by the loose talk that he decided to cooperate in any way he could.

Over Christmas, Peers and a few staff members flew to South Vietnam, and the general made a tour of My Lai 4 and also interviewed a number of Vietnamese officers and survivors about the massacre. He was accompanied during his ground observation by Sergeant Nguyen Dinh Phu, who had served as an interpreter for Captain Medina's company on March 16. After hearing and reading thousands of words about the deep drainage ditch filled with Vietnamese bodies in March, 1968, they found it, twenty-two months later, full of mud, monsoon rainwater, discarded C-ration boxes and soda-pop cans—the residue of an American infantry unit that had passed through a few days before. The bodies of the victims had been pulled out by the Viet Cong for burial. Peers also flew over the Co Luy hamlets to the southeast of My Lai 4. Before leaving for Vietnam he had begun hearing testimony about more shootings in the Co Luy area by Task Force Barker that day. The unit in question was Bravo Company, 4th Battalion, 3rd Infantry, which had served as a blocking force two miles to the east of My Lai 4.

By mid-February the Panel, now divided into three interrogation teams, had quizzed fifty members of Bravo Company, and was beginning to talk to members of the third company in Task Force Barker—Alpha Company, 3rd Battalion, 1st Infantry, which had been in a blocking position north of My Lai 4. The mission of both Bravo and Alpha Companies was to prevent the expected Viet Cong from fleeing the attack initiated by Charlie Company in the village itself.

Just how the second massacre became known to the Panel isn't clear; Charlie Company members, in interviews, said they knew nothing of other shootings. On February 12, 1970, the Army announced that it had charged an infantry

captain with the unpremeditated murder of Vietnamese civilians in the Song My area of Vietnam on March 16, 1968.
The suspect, Captain Thomas K. Willingham of Newark,
New Jersey, was a lieutenant with Bravo Company at the
time of the offense. Sources told newsmen he was accused of
either killing or ordering the killing of up to twenty Vietnamese. The case was distinct from the My Lai 4 slayings in
that Willingham was not charged with premeditated murder.

One possible source for the Panel's information could
have been the pilots and crewmen of the two aviation support units that were over My Lai 4 and the area on March
16. By February 4 Peers systematically had interviewed
forty of those men, just as he had also interviewed three of
the chaplains attached to the Americal Division—the men
to whom any GI with a stricken conscience might have
turned.

One helicopter crewman was convinced he told the Panel
more than they wanted to believe. Larry Colburn, who was
aboard Warrant Officer Thompson's aircraft that day, testified in January about his visit to Colonel Henderson after
the mission. "They seemed pretty surprised. Somebody said,
'Well, we don't think you did see him.' They tried to convince me, sort of, that I saw Barker." Colburn said the
Panel, after trying to suggest that it was the deceased Task
Force commander, also said that his visit took place two or
three days after the mission, rather than within hours.
Colburn was mystified by the group's reaction.

By the close of witness interrogations in March, however,
and with the charges laid against Willingham, it was clear
that the Army had chosen well when it picked Peers. The
Panel had accumulated more than 20,000 pages of testimony in four months of grueling work.

For attorneys trying to protect former Charlie Company
members, however, the Panel posed a set of very delicate

problems. The Army and the C.I.D. were refusing civilian attorneys access to statements against their clients, and did not even want to provide copies of any self-incriminating statements. Most of the initial Inspector General and C.I.D. statements had been taken without benefit of counsel, and certainly some of the former GIs, awed by the presence of a colonel or some other high-ranking officer, had less than a perfect understanding of their right to say nothing self-incriminating before submitting to an interrogation. Colonel Wilson, who conducted most of the initial interviews, even admitted in February that he had not fully briefed each potential witness on his rights. "I was told not to," he said in a brief telephone conversation, adding that "everything was completely thought out." The colonel refused to confirm or deny the possibility that some members of Charlie Company had been unofficially granted immunity to testify against others.

Immunity could not be granted by the Peers Panel, but it did have the power—not fully understood by all who testified before it—to file charges against a suspect. If witnesses could not be compelled to testify, the Peers Panel did find various means to encourage them to do so.

In mid-January, Colonel Robert E. Miller of the Panel told Armand Derfner of Jackson, Mississippi, an attorney representing Vernado Simpson, that he could get a copy of Simpson's initial testimony to the Inspector General and C.I.D., and other possibly incriminating statements, if the ex-GI came to Washington prepared to testify before the panel. Simpson, it was explained, would be given an opportunity to study the statements before testifying—and even then could leave the hearing room without saying a word, if he chose.

Derfner's potential defense problems were already complicated by the fact that Simpson had said publicly that he killed eight or ten Vietnamese civilians on March 16, 1968; the lawyer's inability to get relevent testimony given to the Inspector General and the C.I.D. about his client made matters worse. The opportunity to get a look at the statements making up the Army's potential case against his client was tempting, but also a little dangerous. The lawyer, who has had considerable experience in civil rights work in Mississippi, complained that the Peers Panel could give a false sense of security to witnesses. "There's a sort of 'come on, tell us what's going on' atmosphere," Derfner said. "It's the same pattern as in criminal law. People who know what their rights are and know how to ask for them can get protected, and people who don't know what they are aren't told."

The C.I.D., meanwhile, was continuing its separate criminal investigation of the My Lai 4 incident, and those GIs still in the service who had been charged with premeditated murder and other offenses were transferred to Fort McPherson near Atlanta, Georgia, where a series of joint courts-martial was being planned.

There was an additional change in procedure. In late 1969, after some criticism over the wording of the specifications against Calley, Colonel William J. Chilcoat, chief of military justice for the Army, told his staff that in future criminal charges relating to My Lai 4, the victims were just to be described as "human beings," and not as "Oriental human beings."

14

"I Gave Them a Good Boy"

SOME mothers saw it first. Their sons—the men
of Charlie Company—had changed. They jumped
when front doors slammed. They slept fitfully. They
talked little.

Mrs. Anthony Meadlo remembered that when
Paul came home, "he looked like he had just been
whipped. He was so nervous he couldn't even hold
a cup in his hand. He couldn't even eat." Occasionally the youth would cry in shame over what he had
been ordered to do in My Lai 4; at other times he
would brag about how many gooks he had killed
that day. "I gave them a good boy," Mrs. Meadlo
said, "and they made him a murderer."

Kenneth Schiel of Swartz Creek, Michigan, entered the Army immediately after graduation from
high school. He was a small, sensitive youth who
once tore up his driver's license in horror and revulsion after watching three children get killed in a traffic accident. He was serving as a tunnel rat for

Charlie Company on March 16, 1968. When he returned home, his mother recalled: "He wouldn't say much about Vietnam"; a former girl friend remembered hearing him talk only of his buddies who had been killed. But he had written his mother earlier in anguish about an operation in which his unit had destroyed a village, and complained that the company had been ordered to kill civilians. Upon his discharge in March, 1969, the Army suggested that the youth get psychiatric help. Schiel went through five part-time jobs in the next five months, then reenlisted after breaking up with his girl friend. "Why can't they just leave him alone?" his mother, in tears, asked later. "I don't understand. I just know he's my son and I love him."

Some mothers blamed the press and the government for their sons' anxieties. "What the hell's the matter with America?" angrily exclaimed Mrs. George Mauro of Brooklyn, whose son, Robert, had served in Calley's platoon. "There were orders given all around. These boys didn't sit in Saigon in an office. They fought for their country. This is the cream of the crop, and now we are persecuting them. My son still doesn't tell me a thing," Mrs. Mauro added. "He still is nervous." She was particularly angry about *Life* magazine's publication of the Haeberle photographs. "They can't prove to me that this happened. There's dead bodies all over Vietnam. They can't convince me that these pictures were taken in Vietnam."

Mrs. Bruce Cox of Buffalo, New York, felt the same way. "So what if a few Vietnamese got shot? They've killed 40,-000 of our boys over there." She added, however, that her son, Bucky, who was in the third platoon, "said he only saw two dead people. He said nothing about a massacre."

Mrs. Mattie Smith of Chicago had thought her son, Gerald, would have a lot to say when he returned from Vietnam, but she was disappointed: "He was just exhausted. All he did was rest and play music." Gerald A. Smith was charged with premeditated murder and indecent assault in early January, 1970, for his role in the massacre of My Lai 4. His mother found it hard to understand. "He was never in trouble with the police when he was at home. When he went into the Army, he joined because he wanted to finish high school and learn some courses that would help him get a good job," she said. "All he wanted was to get out of the Army, get a decent job and work."

Allen Boyce went into the Army "thinking it might help me get together. It more mixed me up than anything." He told investigators for the C.I.D. that he wanted them "to get to the bottom of this and figure it out." What Charlie Company had done in My Lai 4, he knew, was "sure no way to end the war."

No matter what private feelings the men of Charlie Company might have shared, most of them went back to their old jobs—in construction, as auto mechanics, hauling garbage in a big city, selling shoes—and tried to forget everything about Vietnam. The men coped with their emotions simply by burying them; but it would all resurface in November, 1969, as the nightly TV news and daily newspapers reported about My Lai 4. Almost all of Charlie Company, despite warnings by military officials and civilian lawyers, talked about it in interviews. There was a persistent feeling of shame. "Don't mention my name," one GI asked after an interview. "I don't want people around here pointing to me when I walk down the street, saying, 'There goes that storm trooper.' "

Robert J. Lee of Oshkosh, Wisconsin, was one of Charlie Company's medics at the time of My Lai 4; the GIs called him "Doc." Now he works as a hospital orderly in his hometown, and he doesn't want to talk—or think—about what happened. "I just want to forget it; I don't want to remember," he said. His sense of remorse—heightened perhaps by his training—was strong. "It was the worst thing that ever happened to me. Only my wife and parents know about it— that's all I've told." The other medic in Charlie Company, Nicholas Capezza of New York, was attached to Medina's command post on March 16, 1968. He insisted he saw nothing unusual that day and complained that the news media was "blowing it all out of proportion. To me, it was just like another day in Vietnam. Something like this is always happening. If you really wanted to find stories, you could find fifteen or twenty that could make this look like a nursery rhyme."

Henry Pedrick also insisted during a long interview that there was nothing unusual that day. "I didn't think very much about it," he kept saying. "I didn't have feelings toward it one way or another." He became disturbed, however, when he was told that the Haeberle photographs would be published in *Life* magazine. "They shouldn't do that, they shouldn't do that," he said.

Gregory Olsen told the C.I.D. when they quizzed him in late August: "It was a lot to bottle up and I feel better now that I have talked about it. Even if I was not involved in the killing, I still have a feeling of guilt for not stopping it or not reporting it to Colonel Barker . . . without a doubt I feel Lieutenant Calley was responsible for the shooting. Either him or the Army for letting him go through OCS. I do not condone the shooting of the civilians by members of Company C. They should have refused. To this day I do not know what came over them by not refusing."

For one ex-GI, there was near-tragedy. After glibly telling newsmen about his role in the massacre, he lost his job, left his home, and one morning attempted to swallow a bottle of aspirins. He was hospitalized and recovered.

Others didn't need reminders in daily newspapers. "I knew

it wasn't right," Rennard Doines said, "but over there it makes no difference. I've thought about it since I got back." For a while William Wyatt just stopped believing everything he had seen in Vietnam. "When you come back, it's just like there was some sort of fantasy-land over there." But even so, he added, "I know it wasn't like it was supposed to be."

Charles West wasn't troubled by My Lai 4 while he was in uniform. "Now that I'm a civilian," he said later, "I think like a civilian. I knew that after we got in there and didn't meet resistance, that the mission should have been stopped."

A few GIs—only a few—seemed totally unmoved by the massacre, even in retrospect. "I haven't let it bother me," John Smail insisted. "I never wanted to go there [Vietnam] in the first place. I hated those people, I really did." A member of the third platoon, he had arrived at the hamlet moments after most of the shooting was over, he said. "You know what I thought? Good. I didn't care nothing about the Vietnamese."

Smail also was one of the few Charlie Company members to talk frankly about rape. Most of the company knew there were rapes that day in March, but remained reluctant to talk about them—in war, rape is never justifiable. "That's an everyday affair," Smail said. "You can nail just about everybody on that—at least once. The guys are human, man." By mid-March, 1970, at least three members of Charlie Company were formally accused of rape in connection with the massacre.

Lieutenant Calley nearly broke down after Sergeant Mitchell was charged with assault with intent to murder. He wanted to take the full responsibility, in public, for all of the crimes being laid against Charlie Company, if it would help his commanding officer and his men and exonerate the Army. "He's giving me fits," his attorney, George Latimer, said later. "He's loyal. He doesn't want to embarrass the Army, and it wants to hang him." Calley's attitude didn't change even after the Army stripped him of his Vietnam decorations, including two Bronze Stars, and shifted him from a training job to a meaningless clerical task at base headquarters. He remained loyal as the court-martial neared and Latimer was unsuccessful in a series of legal maneuvers in January and February, 1970, to get the case dismissed. "He wants to hang," an officer friend said. The lieutenant was showing increasing signs of tension. He lost weight, and another friend was shocked when, while drinking beer, Calley suddenly dashed into a bathroom and vomited blood. He explained that he hadn't been able to keep food in his stomach for days and had been drinking beer instead.

For a few GIs, the experience at My Lai 4 changed their former outlook on life; they became increasingly critical about the way the war was being conducted. "I was a candidate for the Minutemen before this," Michael Bernhardt said. "Now I'm all turned around." He had felt no remorse for the Vietnamese civilians while watching them get slaughtered, but he had thought that perhaps he was the odd one. "Maybe this was the way wars really were," he later explained. "Maybe what we saw in the movies and on TV wasn't so, that war was running around and shooting civilians and doing this kind of thing. Maybe all along everybody else knew. I felt like I was left out, like maybe they forgot to tell me something, that this was the way we fought wars and everybody knew but me."

Herbert Carter shot himself in the foot, perhaps to get out of My Lai 4. For him, there was no later sense of personal shame, only a feeling of amazement and irony at the response to the event. "I still wonder why human beings claim to be human beings but still conduct themselves as savages and barbarians," he said. "The United States is supposed to be a peace-loving country; yet they tell them to do something and then they want to hang them for it."

As far as he was concerned, Carter said, what happened at My Lai 4 was not a massacre, but a logical result of the war in Vietnam: "The people didn't know what they were dying for and the guys didn't know why they were shooting them."

Notes

Note: Unless otherwise specified, all interviews cited herein were conducted by the author.

1. "You Wouldn't Believe It"

A basic source for U.S. operations in Quang Ngai Province was *The Military Half,* by Jonathan Schell (New York, Vintage Books, 1968), which was first published in *The New Yorker.* See Schell's letter on Quang Ngai in *The New York Times,* November 26, 1969, for his reaction to My Lai 4. The 1965 marine attack in Quang Ngai ("Operation Starlight") is noted in *Newsweek* for December 8, 1969. Also see Keyes Beech's analysis of Quang Ngai, "Why in Pinkville?" *Chicago Daily News,* November 25, 1969. The quote about sterilizing areas of South Vietnam can be found in "Saigon: the Strategy Gap," by John Hughes, *Christian Science Monitor,* January 22, 1966. *The Military Half* discusses free-fire zones in detail.

The information on Task Force Oregon's evolution into the Americal Division and the problems therein was assembled in interviews with former officers of both units. For information on civilian casualties in South Vietnam, see hearings into "Civilian Casualty, Social Welfare and Refugee Problems in South

Vietnam," *Senate Judiciary Subcommittee to Investigate Problems Connected with Refugees and Escapees,* May 10, 18, August 16, September 21, October 9, 10, 11, 13 and 16, 1967, (Washington: U.S. Government Printing Office); and June 24, 25, 1969 (Washington: U.S. Government Printing Office). The quote about "dogfaces" was made in a Pentagon interview in December, 1969. The quote about being at war with ten-year-old children can be found in "G.I.'s Near Songmy Doubt Any Massacre," by Henry Kamm, *The New York Times,* December 1, 1969.

Miss Claire Culhane's description of GI attitudes toward the Vietnamese can be found in her unpublished *Diary,* kept while she was in Quang Ngai Province and available from her at 6876 Sherbrooke Street, West, No. 20, Montreal 262, Quebec, Canada. Dr. Gordon S. Livingston, Baltimore, Maryland, who formerly served with Colonel Patton in South Vietnam, told of the prejudice of U.S. hospital officials in the *Saturday Review,* September 20, 1969. An excellent report on the hostility of Americans to the Vietnamese was published in *Newsweek,* December 1, 1969. U.S. atrocities in Vietnam were discussed much earlier by sociologist Charles C. Moskos, Jr.; see the December 6, 1965, report in the *Chicago Daily News:* "Heat of Battle Blamed for Viet War Atrocities," by Philip M. Boffey.

The U.S. commander's lament about killing was made to Peter Arnett and Horst Faas of the Associated Press, and can be found in their subsequent story in the *Cleveland Plain Dealer,* January 4, 1970. The material on Colonel Patton comes from "General Abrams Deserves a Better War," by Kevin P. Buckley, *The New York Times Magazine,* October 5, 1969. The military physician quoted is Dr. Gordon Livingston. The cited Pentagon letter was dated October 30, 1969, and signed by Major General William A. Becker, Chief of Legislative Liaison for the Army.

The British photographer's comment can be found in "A Conventional Atrocity," *Sunday Times of London,* November 23, 1969. The GI's letter home was published in the Akron, Ohio, *Beacon Journal* on March 27, 1967, and cited in *In the Name of America,* a study of U.S. military behavior in Vietnam published in 1968 by the Clergy and Laymen Concerned About

Vietnam. Terry Reid's account of action in the 11th Brigade was published by *The Paper,* a daily newspaper serving Central Wisconsin: "Fond du Lac GI says Viet Slaughter 'Common,'" by Allen Ekvall. The GI's closing comment to Schell can be found on page 43 of *The Military Half.*

2. Charlie Company

Captain Medina provided details on his personal background, his role in the training and development of Charlie Company and his actions on March 16, 1968, in a series of personal appearances and interviews beginning with a news conference December 4, 1969, at the Pentagon. For a partial transcript of the news session, see the *Washington Star* for December 5. Medina was interviewed hours after his news conference by Mike Wallace of CBS radio and television, and that interview was broadcast on December 5; a transcript may be available from CBS. On December 6 the captain was interviewed at length at his home in Fort Benning, Georgia, by Peter Braestrup, military writer for the *Washington Post.* A subsequent account of Medina's actions—the most complete published up to then—was printed December 8 in the *Post. The New York Times* interviewed Medina in Washington early the next week and that account was published December 11. The most thorough account of Calley's background was published November 28, 1969, by the *Miami Herald*: "Rusty Calley: The Man Remains a Mystery," by David Nelson. Also see "Boyhood Friends Recall Calley as a Clean-Cut, Popular Youth," by Richard Harwood, in the *Washington Post,* November 30, 1969. Other details of Medina's youth can be found in "Medina Goes Before House Probers Today," by Peter Braestrup, *Washington Post,* December 9, 1969.

Henry Pedrick, Jr., was interviewed by the author on November 20, 1969, at his home in Alameda, California. Michael Bernhardt of Franklin Square, New York, was interviewed at his Army duty station at Fort Dix, New Jersey, on November 18, 1969, and again in a Long Island restaurant near his home on December 6. In addition, there were telephone interviews

December 5, 1969, and February 3, 1970. For a brilliant account of Bernhardt's reaction to My Lai 4, see "The Story of a
Soldier Who Refused to Fire at Songmy," by Joseph Lelyveld,
The New York Times Magazine, December 14, 1969. William
Wyatt was interviewed at his Oklahoma City home January 1,
1970. Calley was interviewed at his quarters in Fort Benning
on November 10, 1969. Sergeant Isaiah Cowen was interviewed
at his home at Columbia, South Carolina, on December 7, 1969.

Allen Boyce was interviewed in his apartment at Bradley
Beach, New Jersey, on December 26, 1969; and subsequently
by telephone. Rennard Doines was interviewed at his sister's
home in Fort Worth, Texas, on January 1, 1969. Charles W.
Hall was interviewed at his Columbus, Ohio, home on November 29, 1969, and by telephone on December 6. Gary Garfolo
was interviewed at his grandmother's home in Stockton, California, on January 29, 1970. Roy L. Wood was interviewed at
his Richmond, Virginia, home on January 9, 1970, and again
by telephone. Robert E. Maples of Freehold, New Jersey, was
interviewed in a Freehold restaurant on December 26, 1969,
and again in Washington, D.C., on January 23, 1970. Daniel E.
Ziegler was interviewed by telephone at Santa Barbara, California, on January 3, 1970, and again on January 18. A thorough account of Sergeant David Mitchell's role in Charlie Company was published December 14, 1969, in the *Cleveland Plain
Dealer*: " 'Acted on Orders' My Lai GI Says," by Joseph Eszterhas. Harry Stanley of Gulfport, Mississippi, was interviewed
in Washington on January 23, 1970, and again by telephone at
his mother's home in Chicago.

Herbert Carter of Houston, Texas, was interviewed in Houston on New Year's Eve, 1969, and again by telephone. Ronald
Grzesik was interviewed at his lawyer's office in Holyoke,
Massachusetts, on January 16, 1970, and later by telephone.
Gregory Olsen of Portland, Oregon, was initially interviewed
at his duty station at Fort Lewis, Washington, on November
21. A second interview was held November 26 at his home in
Portland; and there were many subsequent telephone interviews. James R. Bergthold of Niagara Falls, New York, gave
an interview to the *Niagara Falls Gazette* on November 26,
1969; he was subsequently interviewed at his home on January

4, 1970. Eusebio B. Santellana was interviewed at his San Antonio, Texas, home on January 1, 1970. Gary Crossley of San Marcos, Texas, was interviewed by telephone on February 16, 1970. Charles A. West of Chicago was interviewed in a restaurant there on January 2, 1970; a previous interview with the *Chicago Sun-Times* appeared November 22, 1969. William Doherty of Reading, Massachusetts, was interviewed by telephone at his quarters at Fort Hood, Texas, on November 22, 1970. Richard Pendleton was interviewed January 30, 1970, at his home in Richmond, California.

Michael Terry was interviewed at his Orem, Utah, home on November 17, 1969. Charles Sledge was interviewed in Batesville, Mississippi, his home, on January 3, 1970. John T. Paul was interviewed at a Cherry Hills, New Jersey, restaurant near his home on January 23, 1970. Paul Meadlo was interviewed at his mother's home in New Goshen, Indiana, near Terre Haute, on February 21 and 23, 1969. Charles West's description of his platoon's anger after Sergeant Cox's death came from a *Life* article cited herein. Gregory Olsen's letter to his father was copyrighted by Dispatch News Service on December 2, 1969. The confusion over hamlet and village names described in the footnote was discussed by Richard Hammer in a *Look* article February 10, 1970: "My Lai: Did American Troops Attack the Wrong Place?" Hammer concluded that Medina and his men may have invaded the wrong hamlet. The recollections of Sergeant Nguyen Dinh Phu were initially provided to South Vietnam Senator Tran Van Don during his later investigation of My Lai 4, and relayed by the senator during an interview in Washington on February 13, 1970.

3. The Day—Part I

There are a number of overall accounts of the events on March 16, 1968. See "A 'Real Tight' Company and Its Tests at Songmy," by Peter Kihss, in *The New York Times,* November 30; "A Chicago GI's Pinkville Story: Told to Destroy It," by William Granger and William Braden, the *Chicago Sun-Times,* November 22, 1969; the five Dispatch News Service stories on

My Lai 4, published November 13, 20, 25, December 2 and 9, 1969, in the *Chicago Sun-Times,* among others; "Pinkville Mission Became Death Orgy," by Joseph Eszterhas, *Cleveland Plain Dealer,* December 1, 1969; "The Massacre at Mylai," *Life,* December 5, 1969; and cover stories on My Lai 4 by *Time* on December 5, 1969, and *Newsweek* on December 8, 1969.

For the Vietnamese view, see "Vietnamese Say G.I.'s Slew 567 in Town," by Henry Kamm, *The New York Times,* November 16, 1969; "Ex-Vietcong Tell of Helping Survivors Bury Mylai Dead," by David Hoffman, *Washington Post,* November 30, 1969; "My Lai Civilian Casualties Between 350 and 400," by Keyes Beech, *Chicago Daily News,* December 1, 1969; "Vietnamese Tell of Slaughter at Pinkville," by Robert Kaiser, *The Paper,* Oshkosh, Wisconsin, December 2, 1969; and " 'Day of Massacre' Recalled by S. Vietnamese Farmer," by David Lamb, UPI, as published in the *Philadelphia Evening Bulletin* of November 18, 1969. A better headline was given Lamb's story by the *Washington Star*: "A Viet Peasant Tells His Story of 'Breakfast Massacre.' "

For an excellent account of the helicopter flight patterns over My Lai 4 on March 16, 1968, see "Where Was Gen. Koster?" by Orr Kelly, *Washington Star,* December 11, 1969. Vernado Simpson, Jr., described his activities at My Lai 4 in an NBC television interview November 25, 1969. See also "Veteran Says He Slew 10 in Vietnam Village," by Roy Reed in *The New York Times,* November 27, 1969. Jay Roberts of Arlington, Virginia, was interviewed December 18, 1969, in a Washington area restaurant, and again by telephone on February 21, 1970. Ronald L. Haeberle's description of his day, "Cameraman Saw GIs Slay 100 Villagers," by Joseph Eszterhas, was published in the *Cleveland Plain Dealer,* November 20, 1969; and also in the above-cited *Life* article.

Sergeant Duong Minh's recollections were also provided to Senator Don in South Vietnam, and relayed by the senator in a Washington interview. Hugh C. Thompson's role in My Lai 4 was initially reported by Ted Sell of the *Los Angeles Times* news service, "Massacre Hero Rescued Child," in the *Phila-*

delphia Inquirer, November 29, 1969. Warrant Officer Hugh Thompson was interrogated for three days at the Pentagon by Colonel William Wilson of the Inspector General staff, June 11–13, 1969. Material and quotations about his role at My Lai 4 were taken from a transcript of that interrogation. Lawrence M. Colburn also was interviewed by Colonel Wilson, on June 19, 1969; he gave subsequent telephone interviews to the author at his home in Mount Vernon, Washington, on February 4 and 16, 1970. The GIs' smoke break was reported by Thompson during one of his Pentagon interviews and subsequently confirmed in interviews with the men of Charlie Company.

4. The Day—Part II

John Kinch's account of Medina's conversation with Colonel Barker was published in *Life,* December 5, 1969. Kinch was still on active duty with the Army in Vietnam at the end of 1969. William C. Lloyd's testimony to the Provost Marshal was given November 10, 1969. Captain Brian W. Livingston's Biblical comment was made December 2, 1969, during an Article 32 hearing at Fort Hood, Texas, on the charges against Sergeant Mitchell. Dennis Conti's testimony to the Criminal Investigating Division was taken October 30, 1969. Harry Stanley was interrogated October 14, 1969. Herbert Carter made his statements November 6, 1969. Charles Gruver of Tulsa, Oklahoma, was initially interviewed on November 22, 1969, by Robert Ray of KWTV, a CBS affiliate in Oklahoma City. Gruver later gave a widely distributed interview to the AP; see "Ex-GI Recalls Village Attack," *Washington Star,* November 24, 1969. Gruver was subsequently interviewed briefly by telephone December 5, 1969. Richard Pendleton initially told of the Medina shooting in an interview published November 26, 1969, by the Richmond, California, *Independent:* "Local GI Saw Massacre," by Gary Hanlon. He amplified his recollections in the interview cited herein.

5. Victory

See the above-cited Peter Kihss *New York Times* story for a reference to the first battle report to the Pentagon. Arthur Dunn of Forest Park, Illinois, was interviewed by telephone about January 10, 1970. Dunn also gave an account of his experiences, "Army Story of Pinkville 'Fishy': Ex-GI," by William Currie and Joseph McLaughlin, to the *Chicago Tribune,* November 28, 1969. For various accounts of the division and brigade publications on the My Lai 4 battle, see "Army Account of Pinkville Incident Told," by William Currie and Joseph McLaughlin, *Chicago Tribune,* December 1, 1969, and "Army Reported 128 Enemy Dead at Songmy," UPI in *The New York Times,* November 26, 1969. For the text of the Westmoreland letter of congratulations, see "Pinkville GI Action Hailed Before Probe," by Keyes Beech, *Chicago Daily News,* December 1, 1969.

6. Aftermath

Medina's account of his telephone conversation with Major Calhoun and Major General Koster was given both to Peter Braestrup in the December 8, 1969, *Washington Post* article and to James McCartney of the Knight Newspapers. For McCartney's version, see "Medina Says Top Officer Halted My Lai Body Count," *St. Petersburg Times,* December 12, 1969. Also see "Did General Send Warning Not to Kill My Lai Civilians?" UPI dispatch in the *Chicago Sun-Times,* December 19, 1969. Captain Charlie R. Lewellen was interviewed about his tape recording on February 21, 1970, by telephone at his home in Fort Benning. The existence of the tape was made known during a court hearing in January, 1970. See "Copter Talks Taped at Time of Mylai, Attorney Discloses," by Jim Baker, AP in the *Washington Post,* January 20, 1970. John Kinch's account of the interrogation tactics of Charlie Company was first published in *Life* on December 5, 1969, and confirmed in subsequent interviews with other Charlie Company members. John Smail was interviewed by telephone at his home in Renton, Washington, on February 4, 1970. Ronald L. Ridenhour of Phoenix, Arizona, was initially interviewed November 17, 1969, in a restaurant near his college dormitory at Claremont, California, with many subsequent telephone interviews. He was again questioned in Washington on February 2, 1970.

7. The Cover-Up

Colonel Henderson's promotion to brigade commander was first reported by Fred Farrar of the *Chicago Tribune,* "Brigade Given New Chief Day Before My Lai," January 7, 1970. For Henderson's varying versions of what he did after My Lai 4, see "Only 1 Civilian Killed, GIs Told Brigade Chief," by William McGaffin, *Chicago Daily News,* November 26, 1969; " 'I Didn't Order Pinkville,' Says GI Brigade's Chief," by William McGaffin, *Chicago Daily News,* November 27, 1969; "GI Says Captain Stopped Killing After Radio Message," *Washington Post,* November 28, 1969; and the above-cited *New York Times* article of December 1, 1969. Henderson generally refused to grant radio or television interviews, but TV station WVEC in Hampton, Virginia, did record the officer on tape and UPI moved a summary of that interview on its wires for November 28, 1969. Ron Nessen of NBC summarized the results of an interview with Henderson on the Huntley-Brinkley Show November 27, 1969.

For an overall discussion of the efficacy of the early Henderson probe, see "GIs Cleared in '68 Probe of Massacre," by Peter Braestrup of the *Washington Post,* November 18, 1969. Joseph Reid of Mountain View, California, told of his impressions of the battle during a telephone interview at his home on February 22, 1970. See "Barker Saw Pinkville Battle from Helicopter, 2 ex-GIs Say," by William Currie and James McLaughlin, *Chicago Tribune* November 29, 1969. Army Secretary Resor's summary of the investigation was given to a meeting of the Senate Armed Services Committee on November 26, 1969; the statement was reprinted in full in the next day's *New York Times.* Former Lieutenant John Gore of Lawrence-

ville, New Jersey, was interviewed about the Lewellen tapes
by telephone on February 21, 1970.

An excellent account of the early investigation in Vietnam
can be found in the *Times of London* for November 24;
"Woman Survivor Repeats Story of Killings," by Fred Emery.

For indications of Colonel Khien's dilemma, see "Saigon
Officials Slow to Investigate Massacre Charges," *The New York
Times,* November 20, 1969; "Viet Colonel Doubts GI Atrocity," *Chicago Daily News,* November 17, 1969. The fact that
Thieu had learned of My Lai 4 in 1968 was hinted at by *The
New York Times* on November 19, 1969: "Charge of Massacre
by G.I.s Faces Saigon Inquiry," by Henry Kamm. It was flatly
broadcast December 2, 1969, on the Walter Cronkite CBS
evening news.

James May's denial of knowledge of My Lai 4 was initially
made to Keyes Beech of the *Chicago Daily News,* December 4,
1969: "U.S. Adviser in Area Knew Nothing of Viet Slaughter,"
and confirmed in a telephone interview at his State Department
office on January 16, 1970. Robert Burke was interviewed by
telephone at his station in the Naval War College, Newport,
Rhode Island, on January 17, 1970.

8. The Uncovering—Part I

The French reports of the massacre that were published in 1968
were revealed by Jacques Decornoy in *Le Monde Weekly* for
November 26, 1969: "Getting the Message Home." Ron Ridenhour's role in the My Lai 4 incident has been well and often
told by the news media. See in particular " 'My Job Is Done,'
Says Veteran Who Broke the Story," by Laurence Stern, *Washington Post,* November 30, 1969; " 'Dark, Bloody' Tale Had
to Be Reported," by Bob Warden, *Chicago Daily News* wire
service as published in the *Philadelphia Inquirer,* November
25, 1969; "My Lai Massacre: Grim Details, Unanswered Questions," by Peter Harkness, *Congressional Quarterly,* December
5, 1969; "He Broke the Story of the Mylai 'Massacre,' " by
Lloyd Shearer, *Parade,* January 18, 1970; and "Congress,
Three Magazines Passed Up Pinkville Story," by Peter Brae-

strup and Richard Homan, *Washington Post* wire service story as published in the *Chicago Sun-Times,* November 22, 1969.

Arthur Orman was interviewed by telephone in Phoenix in late January, 1970. The Reverend Latch's statement about the Ridenhour letter can be found in the *Congressional Quarterly* issue cited above. John R. Blandford of the House Armed Services Committee was interviewed by telephone February 12, 1970. Roger Lewis and Representative Udall were interviewed by telephone January 26, 1970. Secretary of Defense Laird's statement about Ridenhour's letter came during an impromptu news conference December 1, 1969, at the Pentagon. See "Laird Doubts Peace Plan Hurt by Case," *Washington Post,* December 2, 1969.

For another view of the chain of events that initiated the investigation, see "Udall Says Rivers Aided Mylai Probe," by Laurence Stern, *Washington Post,* December 4, 1969. Details on Colonel Wilson's movements were gathered from interviews and a close reading of all other available material. For example, Medina mentioned the date of Wilson's interrogation during his interview with Braestrup of the *Washington Post,* published December 8, 1969. Michael Cunningham, Ridenhour's agent, was interviewed December 25, 1969, and January 22, 1970. For his view of what happened, see "Hartford Man 'Sat On' Original Massacre Story," by John Sherman, *Hartford Courant,* December 7, 1969.

9. The Uncovering—Part II

The statistics on the total number of witnesses interrogated by Wilson came from the Resor report to Congress November 26, 1969, cited above. The "flagging" of Calley's records was revealed by Colonel Kiersey during testimony in February at a pretrial hearing at Fort Benning, Georgia. See "Colonel Tells of 'Hold' in Investigating Calley," by James Doyle, *Washington Star,* February 11, 1970. See Resor's statement for the date of the submission of Wilson's report to General Westmoreland.

Haeberle's experiences with his photographs are described

by him in the December 20, 1969, *Cleveland Plain Dealer* interview cited above. Further information was supplied by Jay Roberts in an interview. George Latimer was interviewed a number of times, by telephone and at his Salt Lake City, Utah, office, beginning October 27, 1969, and ending January 29, 1970. Colonel Wilson's flight to Fort Benning in August to brief the officers there was also brought out at the pretrial hearing for Calley in February, as were the subsequent details of the attempt by young officers to override what they thought would be a political decision to not prosecute Calley. Coverage of the hearing between February 9 and 12, 1970, was extensive in the *Washington Star, Washington Post, Chicago Tribune, The New York Times,* and New York *Daily News.*

Nixon's anger at the Army's delay in investigating the massacre was reported by Hugh Sidey, in his column "The Presidency," in *Life,* December 12, 1969. Also see "Nixon Told of Pinkville by Sec. Laird Last August," by Thomas B. Ross, *Chicago Sun-Times,* December 4, 1969. A chronology of events in the unfolding of the My Lai 4 massacre expressing the view of the House Armed Services Committee is available from the Committee; it can also be found in the above-cited *Congressional Quarterly* issue. UPI moved the full text of the summary on its wires December 5, 1969.

10. The Press

The original Army release is available from the Pentagon and the Fort Benning public information office. For an account of Charles Black's role in developing the story, see "Here Is How the Story Unfolded," by J. D. Quigg, *Editor & Publisher* magazine, December 13, 1969. Arnold Markowitz of the *Miami Herald* was interviewed by telephone in early February.

Laird's close monitoring of the wire services was revealed at his December 1, 1969, news conference, and reported by the *Washington Post* the next day.

Senator Stennis issued a statement November 26, 1969, telling of his Committee's private briefing; it was reprinted in *The New York Times* on November 27, 1969. For Westmoreland's remarks to the Association of the U.S. Army, see " 'Massacre' Puts Army on Trial," by Orr Kelly, *Washington Star,* December 2, 1969.

The quote from George Latimer before news of My Lai 4 was publicly known appeared in the *Washington Post,* November 13, 1969: "U.S. Officer Is Accused of Mass Viet 'Murders,' " by Peter Braestrup. The account of the author's role in developing the My Lai 4 story is told more fully in the Spring, 1970, issue of the *Columbia Journalism Review,* in the "Notes on the Art" section. Henry Kamm's efforts to reach the survivors of My Lai 4 was told to Marsh Clark of *Time*'s Saigon bureau; a copy of Clark's file was made available to the author. For the *Washington Post*'s denigration of the story, see "Pentagon Says Viet Killings Exaggerated," November 17, 1969. Ridenhour was called a "tipster" in the San Francisco *Sunday Examiner & Chronicle,* November 26, 1969.

For the debate in London over My Lai 4, see any London newspaper for November 20 through 25, 1969. The headline in the *Daily Sketch* was cited by Anthony Lewis in *The New York Times* on November 20, 1969: "Wilson Sees 'Grave Atrocities' If Massacre Reports Are True." The *Washington Post* article that tended to emphasize the hardships suffered by Charlie Company was "Frustration Could Have Caused Alleged Killings," by Peter Braestrup, November 22, 1969. The similarly cited AP dispatch was "Even Vietnamese Children Could Terrorize the GIs," by John T. Wheeler, appearing in the *Washington Star,* December 5, 1969. General Eaker's column, "When Is Act of War Called a Massacre?" was published December 22, 1969, in the *Detroit News.* The AP report of the new finding of documents can be found in the *Washington Post* for November 24, 1969: The story was leaked earlier to Joseph Fried of the New York *Daily News*; see "Hue Massacre Pinned on Reds," November 23, 1969. The documents also were treated seriously by the *Christian Science Monitor*'s George W. Ashworth: "Hue Massacre Detailed in Report," December 1, 1969.

A full transcript of Paul Meadlo's CBS interview was published on November 25, 1969, in both the *Washington Post* and *New York Times.* The Stern-Harwood column, "Pinkville

Symbolizes Brutalization That Inevitably Affects Men at War,"
was published November 26, 1969, in the *Washington Post*.
The AP reporter who finally wrote in 1969 of a 1965 massacre
was John Wheeler in the dispatch cited above. The other AP
dispatch cited was "Impact of My Lai Assessed," by Horst
Faas and Peter Arnett, in the *Washington Star*, December 8,
1969. A good summary of press reaction in the wake of
Meadlo's appearance was carried Monday morning, December
1, 1969, by UPI.

For a good example of turnabout, see "Atrocities Cast Pall
over U.S.," by Ted Lewis, New York *Daily News*, November
28, 1969. The editorial cited from the *Philadelphia Inquirer*
appeared November 26, 1969. The *Washington Star* editorial
was published the same day. Ray Cromley's syndicated column
appeared November 28, 1969, in the *Washington News*. The
National Observer editorial was printed December 1, 1969.
Newsweek, Time, and *Life* published their best material on
My Lai 4 in early December, 1969, as noted above. Ridenhour
was *The New York Times'* "Man in the News" on November
29, 1969: "Pinkville Gadfly," by Christopher Lydon. Colonel
Henderson's comment was given to the *Washington Post* and
published in the above-cited November 28, 1969, article.

11. Vietnam Reacts

For the initial denial that anything at all happened in My Lai 4,
see "No Evidence of Mass Killing by Yanks, S. Viet Official
Declares," by Richard Pyle of the Associated Press, as published in the *Salt Lake Tribune*, November 18, 1969. The end
of censorship in South Vietnamese newspapers was reported by
Reuters, "Saigon Press Breaks Quiet on 'Pinkville,'" in the
Washington Post, November 21, 1969.

The denial of the massacre charges based on General Lam's
study was prominently reported: see "South Vietnam Denies
'Massacre' by GI's," by Orr Kelly, *Washington Star*, November
22, 1969, and "Massacre Story False, Saigon Says," *Washington Post*, November 23, 1969. The quote from American officials appeared in Orr Kelly's story.

Senator Don's inquiry was most thoroughly reported in *The New York Times* throughout. See "Foe of Thieu Sets Massacre Inquiry," by Henry Kamm, November 26, 1969; and "Saigon's Senate Will Investigate Alleged Atrocity," also by Kamm, November 28, 1969. The *Chinh Luan* editorial was cited by Kamm. For the demonstrations of public unrest over My Lai 4, see "Catholic Ire over Pinkville," UPI dispatch in the *Chicago Sun-Times,* December 1, 1969. Marshal Ky's emerging role and Senator Don's field trip to My Lai 4 and Quang Ngai City were reported most thoroughly by *The New York Times* from November 29, 1969, through December 7, 1969. In particular, see "Three Saigon Senators Report Signs Civilians Were Slain at Close Range," in the *Times* on December 4, 1969. Senator Don also was interviewed by the author, date cited above, on his investigation.

The preliminary Senate Committee conclusions were reported in *The New York Times,* "Saigon Senator Report on Songmy," by James P. Sterba, December 16, 1969; a similar House Committee study of My Lai 4 was reported in the *Washington Post,* "Songmy Data Is Termed Insufficient," by David Hoffman, December 18, 1969.

The footnote dealing with the alleged atrocity in Co Luy was based on the above-cited *Times of London* story by Fred Emery. Senator Don's final conclusions were widely reported in U.S. newspapers and on television: see "Saigon Senators Declare Songmy 'An Isolated Act,' " by Terence Smith, *The New York Times,* January 5, 1970; and "Saigon Panel Confirms My Lai, Blames Thieu," AP in the *Washington Star,* January 5, 1970. The Buddhist report on the massacre was given little press coverage: an AP dispatch was moved as item 24 on its Washington wire on January 26, 1970, but apparently did not receive much usage by U.S. newspapers.

12. America Reacts

The *Cleveland Plain Dealer* published a story telling of the reaction to the Haeberle photographs on November 21, 1969: "Callers Say PD Shouldn't Have Used Pictures of Civilian

Slaughter in Viet." The reaction to the *Washington Star*'s publication was privately conveyed. *The New York Times* survey
of GIs' reaction was published December 1, 1969: "G.I.s
near Songmy Doubt Any Massacre," by Henry Kamm. Calley's
initial support from the American Legion was thoroughly reported by the *Columbus* (Georgia) *Enquirer,* in December and
thereafter. James Smith's activities on behalf of Calley were
included in a *Washington Star* story on December 15, 1969:
"Probe Calls Gen. Koster on My Lai," by Orr Kelly. Other
accounts appeared in the *Atlanta Constitution.* The AP reported on December 20 that Calley had opened a bank account;
see item 112 on its Washington wire for that date. For Calley's
status with used-car dealers, see "Off Base, Calley a Celebrity,"
Washington Star, February 11, 1970. For Calley's meeting
with Governor Wallace, see "Calley Hears Praise as He Visits
Wallace," by J. M. McFadden in the *Washington Post,* February 22, 1970. Many other newspapers also reported the visit.
The *Minneapolis Tribune* poll was reported December 22,
1969, in the *Washington Post*: "Poll Finds Doubters on My
Lai." The *Time* poll was published in its January 9, 1970, issue;
see "Most Back Calley in a Poll for *Time,*" *The New York
Times,* January 5, 1970. Deputy Secretary Packard's poll of
South Vietnamese opinion was revealed to newsmen December
5, 1969, at a Pentagon briefing; the AP reported Packard's
statements as item 123 on its Washington wire that day.

Calley's fund-raising help from the American Legion was
widely reported: see "Legion to Raise Funds for Calley," AP
in the *Washington Post,* January 17, 1970, and "Calley Here
to Discuss Trial Funds," by Bill Middleton, *Jacksonville Times-
Union,* January 16, 1970. The Florida poll cited was conducted
by the *Times-Union* and published January 7, 1970. The comments from Fort Benning officers were made in private interviews.

The GI who suffered after telling of atrocities in Vietnam
was Fred Sedahl, a reporter for the *Savannah* (Georgia) *Morning News.* A UPI account of his plight was published by the
Chicago Sun-Times, December 1, 1969: "Vet's Story Enrages
Readers." Senator Ellender's interview was given to a local
television station in Louisiana on January 15, 1970, and re-

ported by Walter Cronkite the next evening. Senator Hollings' statement was made on the Senate floor November 25, 1969—the day after Meadlo's CBS interview. See page S14979 of the *Congressional Record*. Senator Dominick began his attacks on the same day in the Senate—see S14978 of the *Congressional Record*; he gave at least three major speeches on the news media and Calley over the next two weeks. The December 2 speech can be found on page S15293 of the *Congressional Record*. Representative Foreman's speech can be found on page E10247 of the *Congressional Record* for December 4, 1969. Representative Rarick's attack can be found on page E10237 of the *Congressional Record* of December 4, 1969. The letter to Representative Hogan was placed in the *Congressional Record* on December 29, 1969, at page E11033.

The best account of Ichord's slide show on Hue was "Pentagon Briefs Lawmakers on Hue Massacre," by Richard Homan, *Washington Post,* December 9, 1969. For the House debate on the resolution praising each serviceman, see pp. H12379–81 in the *Congressional Record* for December 15, 1969. Bingham's complaints are therein.

McGovern's television interview took place November 30, 1969, on the CBS show *Face the Nation.* For a scathing commentary on the lack of commentary over My Lai 4, see two columns by Mary McGrory in the *Washington Star*: "Silence Greets Viet Massacres," November 25, 1969, and "Where Our Conscience Died . . . ," November 26, 1969.

For the first Administration reaction to My Lai 4, see "American Aides in Saigon Say U.S. Does Not Condone Atrocities," Reuter's in *The New York Times,* November 20, 1969. The Pentagon spokesman who relayed Laird's action was Richard Capen, an Assistant Secretary of Defense for Public Affairs; it was reported on CBS and NBC network news November 26, 1969, along with the similar denials from Generals Johnson and Westmoreland. The "shocked and sick" quote can be found in "Hill Panels Call Resor on Viet Massacre Case," *Washington Star,* November 26, 1969. The Congressional expressions of shock after viewing Haeberle's slides were widely reported; see any major newspaper for November 27, 1969. Young's quote also was given wide prominence.

Overseas criticism of U.S. policy in Vietnam stemming from My Lai 4 was summarized with differing views by the *Washington Post* on December 1, 1969 ("Mylai Reaction Abroad Is Restrained") and *The New York Times* two days later ("Much of World Views Songmy Affair as an American Tragedy," by Henry Tanner). The State Department pressure for White House action was revealed by James McCartney of Knight Newspapers, writing November 26, 1969, in the *Detroit Free Press:* "Nixon Urged to Decry Massacre." Nixon's November 3 statement about bloodbath and its link to My Lai 4 was commented upon in "War Atrocities and the Law," by William Gerber, *Editorial Research Reports,* No. 1, January 7, 1970.

The Nixon statement abolishing biological warfare was given strong emphasis by newspapers on November 26, 1969; for analysis of his action, see "New CBW Policy Rebuff to Military," by Seymour M. Hersh, *Chicago Sun-Times,* November 30, 1969.

The first White House reaction to My Lai 4 was given predominant newspaper play on November 27, 1969. See "White House Says U.S. Policy Bars Any Mass Slaying," by Robert M. Smith, *The New York Times,* November 27, 1969.

Colonel Kennedy's order restraining comment was issued November 25; a clarified account of its scope was reported by UPI the next day. See "News Media Given Clearance by Army on Any Calley Data," *The New York Times,* November 27, 1969. The Pentagon's attempt to increase speculation about its jurisdiction to try ex-GIs can be traced through the following newspaper articles: "Special War Crimes Panel Weighed to Try Ex-GIs," by John P. MacKenzie, *Washington Post,* November 27, 1969; "Ex-GIs May Face Trial in Massacre," AP in the *Chicago Daily News,* November 28, 1969; "Army Studies How to Try My Lai Ex-GIs," by Charles W. Corddry, *Baltimore Sun,* November 29, 1969; and "Army Looks at Ways to Try Ex-GIs," by Lyle Denniston, *Washington Star,* December 3, 1969. Kennedy's action regarding his ban on speaking out and the subsequent appeal to the Military Court of Appeals were reported fully in most major newspapers on February 1, 2 and 3, 1970.

A transcript of Medina's news conference was partially reprinted in the *Washington Star* on December 5, 1969, as cited above. Kennedy's comment about excepting Medina from his order was made during a later pretrial hearing at Fort Benning; see a combined AP and UPI story in the *Chicago Sun-Times,* December 17, 1969. Nixon's news conference remark about My Lai 4 was reprinted in full in the *Washington Post* and *The New York Times* for December 9, 1969. *The New York Times* article citing the 1967 directive was "Troops Got Order in 1967 to Report Any War Crime," by William Beecher, December 13, 1969. Laird's TV comment on the possibility of trying civilians was made during an interview on *Issues and Answers* over the ABC network on December 14, 1969. Senator Young's criticisms were made on the Senate floor; see page S17006 of the *Congressional Record* for December 17, 1969, and S15333 of the *Congressional Record* for December 2, 1969.

The cited TV appearances by F. Lee Bailey were on January 12, 1970, *Panorama,* broadcast on station WTTG in Washington; and an appearance January 14, 1970, on the evening news with Martin Agronsky on WTOP in Washington (the interview was taped a day before).

L. Mendel Rivers' three-day hearing on My Lai 4 received wide coverage in the press; especially see James Doyle's stories in the *Washington Star* for December 9, 10 and 11, 1969, and his wrap-up article, "Politics and Policy in My Lai Probe," in the *Sunday Star,* December 14, 1969.

The Goodell-Minchell call for an inquiry on My Lai 4 was reported in *The New York Times* of November 21: "Two in Congress Ask Vietnam Massacre Inquiry," by Robert M. Smith. The *Times'* editorial calling for a Congressional investigation was "An American Nightmare," November 22, 1969; the *Daily News* editorial was "Calley—A Case for Congress," November 26, 1969. The Stennis, Humphrey and Goldberg recommendations were made between December 4, 1969, and December 7, 1969, and fully reported at the time; for one story dealing with all of them, see "Stennis, Humphrey Ask Independent Probe of My Lai," AP in the *Washington Star,* December 8, 1969. The ACLU recommendations were best covered by *The New York Times:* "A.C.L.U. Wants Calley Freed Because of Publicity," by Robert M. Smith, December 12, 1969. Joe Kraft's column,

"Anguish at West Point Hints Best Panel for Mylai Inquiry," was published December 9, 1969, in the *Washington Post.* William S. White's column, "Reaction of Public to Mylai Isolates Peace Extremists," appeared in the *Washington Post* December 13, 1969.

13. The Peers Panel

The only newspaper or magazine to comment on the long delay between the initiation of the Army investigation and the establishment of the Peers Panel was the *Nation* in "The Larger Issues," an editorial published December 22, 1969. The announcement of the investigation was reported straightforwardly by the news media: see "Army Will Review Study of '68 on Alleged Killings," by Robert M. Smith, *The New York Times,* November 25, 1969. Thereafter, news coverage was limited to a listing of witnesses before the Panel and announcements of its field trips. No detailed information on the investigation was provided. A mimeographed fact sheet on Peers' background was made available to newsmen by the Pentagon, but for a good description of the general, see "General Leading My Lai Probe Rated Tough, Bluntly Honest," by Jim G. Lucas of Scripps-Howard, as reprinted in the *Washington News,* January 5, 1970.

Six former and present State Department officials were interviewed on a not-for-attribution basis about the Peers appointment. Robert Komer was interviewed by telephone at his offices at the Rand Corporation in Santa Monica, California, in mid-February. General Koster testified December 15 and 16, 1969, before Peers.

MacCrate's news conference was held December 10; see "Candor Pledged on My Lai Probe," by Muriel Dobbin, *Baltimore Sun,* for a typical account. The only reporter to publicly chaff at the tight security around the Panel was Orr Kelly of the *Washington Star;* see "An 'Open' Pentagon Would Be Nice," February 3, 1970. Kesler made his statement January 5, 1970; it was fully reported on the next day by Ted Sell of the *Los Angeles Times* and Orr Kelly of the *Washington Star.* Peers' tour of South Vietnam was fully covered, if routinely, by the wire services. See "Army Investigators Visit Ruins at Mylai," AP in *The New York Times,* January 4, 1970, for an example.

The charges against Willingham were reported in full by *The New York Times,* "Murders at Songmy Charged to Officer with a 2d Company," February 13, 1970. A list of witnesses before the Peers' Panel was carefully kept by Ted Sell, who graciously permitted the author to study it. Armand Derfner was interviewed by telephone at Jackson, Mississippi, on February 13, 1970. The consolidation of the overall My Lai 4 inquiry was reported in *The New York Times* January 14, 1970: "Army Consolidating Songmy Inquiry at Georgia Base." Colonel Chilcoat's orders deleting the "Oriental" in connection with My Lai 4 massacre charges was cited in the *Washington Post* for February 11, 1970: "Nixon's Influence in Case Feared, Calley Hearing Told," by Richard Homan.

14. "I Gave Them a Good Boy"

Mrs. Meadlo was interviewed along with her son in New Goshen, Indiana, on November 21 and 23, 1969. Meadlo's occasional bragging was publicly noted by his mother-in-law, Mrs. May Fuller: "Stand Up and Shoot Him," UPI in the *Chicago Daily News,* November 26, 1969. Kenneth Schiel's letter home and his mother's reactions to his involvement in My Lai 4 were reported in the *Flint* (Michigan) *Journal:* "Swartz Creek GI Being Questioned in Viet 'Massacre,'" November 25, and "Schiel Highly Regarded in Swartz Creek," by William A. James, November 26, 1969.

Mrs. Mauro was interviewed by telephone in Brooklyn on December 26, 1969. Mrs. Bruce Cox was briefly interviewed on January 4, 1970, in her home in suburban Buffalo, New York. Mrs. Mattie Smith told both the *Chicago Daily News* and *Chicago Sun-Times* about her reactions to the charges against her son; see "Accused Soldier 'Was Gentle Type,'" by David Canfield, *Chicago Daily News,* January 9, 1970; and "Bewildered Mother Talks of GI Accused of Murders," by Sam Washington and William Granger, *Chicago Sun-Times,* January 9, 1970.

Robert J. Lee was interviewed briefly by telephone at his home in Oshkosh, Wisconsin, on February 13, 1970. Nicholas Capezza was interviewed by telephone at his home in Queens on February 24, 1970. Gregory Olsen talked to the C.I.D. on August 30, 1969, at Fort Lewis, Washington.

The stripping of Calley's medals was noted in the November 30, 1969, *Washington Post* feature on him cited above. For an overenthusiastic but otherwise accurate account of Calley's new job at Fort Benning, see "Work on Museum Captivates Calley, But War Is Near," by Clarence Jones, *Miami Herald,* November 28, 1969.

Bernhardt's comments were made in an interview and to Joseph Lelyveld in the above-cited *New York Times Magazine* story. Carter's closing quote was made during an interview with him on January 31, 1969.

About the Author

SEYMOUR M. HERSH is the author of *Chemical and Biological Warfare: America's Hidden Arsenal,* which is credited with having a major influence on this country's recent decision to stop production of biological weapons. Mr. Hersh began his journalism career as a police reporter for the city news bureau in Chicago and later covered the Pentagon for the AP. Mr. Hersh, who is thirty-three, was press secretary for Senator Eugene McCarthy early in his campaign for the Democratic Presidential nomination. He won a special George Polk Memorial Award in February, 1970, and the Worth Bingham Prize in March, 1970, for his reporting on the My Lai 4 massacre. He is married and lives in Washington, D.C.